OCR RECOGNISING ACHIEVEMENT

HODDER EDUCATION

Official Publisher Partnership

OCR
iMEDIA

Levels 1 and 2

Kevin Wells

HODDER
EDUCATION
PART OF HACHETTE LIVRE UK

Orders: please contact Bookpoint Ltd, 130 Milton Park, Abingdon, Oxon OX14 4SB.
Telephone: (44) 01235 827720. Fax: (44) 01235 400454. Lines are open from 9.00–5.00,
Monday to Saturday, with a 24 hour message answering service. You can also order
through our website www.hoddereducation.co.uk

If you have any comments to make about this, or any of our other titles, please send them
to educationenquiries@hodder.co.uk

British Library Cataloguing in Publication Data
A catalogue record for this title is available from the British Library

ISBN: 978 0 340 972366

First Edition Published 2008
This Edition Published 2008
Impression number   10 9 8 7 6 5 4 3 2 1
Year   2012 2011 2010 2009 2008

Hachette Livre UK's policy is to use papers that are natural, renewable and recyclable
products and made from wood grown in sustainable forests. The logging and
manufacturing processes are expected to conform to the environmental regulations of the
country of origin.

Cover photo © jamalludin din/Fotolia.com
Typeset by Fakenham Photosetting, Fakenham, Norfolk.
Printed in Italy for Hodder Education, a part of Hachette Livre UK, 338 Euston Road,
London NW1 3BH

Table of Contents

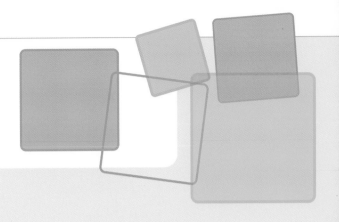

Acknowledgements

The author and publishers would like to thank the following for the use of screenshots in this book.

Microsoft product screenshots reprinted with permission from Microsoft Corporation.

Adobe product screen shots reprinted with permission from Adobe Systems Incorporated.

Screenshots from MissionMaker reproduced by permission of Immersive Education, www.immersiveeducation.com.

Screenshot from Opus Presenter reproduced by permission of Digital Workshop, www.digitalworkshop.com.

Screenshot from CoffeeCup Flash Firestarter reproduced by permission of CoffeeCup Software, www.coffeecup.com.

Every effort has been made to trace and acknowledge ownership of copyright. The publishers will be glad to make suitable arrangements with any copyright holders whom it has not been possible to contact.

Introduction

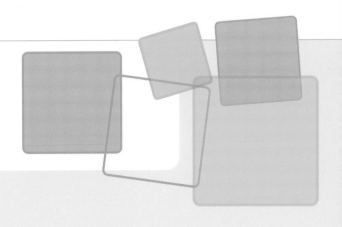

The iMedia qualification bridges the gap between IT and creative media. It builds on your technical skills and encourages your creativity at the same time in producing solutions to meet the needs of a client. The Level 1 and Level 2 Certificate/Diploma in iMedia is a vocational qualification designed to provide a route into a wide range of job roles that use digital media. The purpose of each unit is to develop your skills in the use of equipment and software applications to produce a final piece of work that would satisfy a client brief. The qualification is made up of seven different subject units at Level 1 and eight different subject units at Level 2. By completing either three or five units, you will be awarded a certificate/diploma in iMedia as shown below:

- Certificate in iMedia: Complete *three* units, *one* of which must be Unit 1 (Digital World of Media at Level 1 and Digital Graphics at Level 2)
- Diploma in iMedia: Complete *five* units, *one* of which must be Unit 1 (Digital World of Media at Level 1 and Digital Graphics at Level 2)

Individual units that are completed and passed will earn you a certificate for that single unit. Each unit is a pass or fail with no other grades available. In order to pass each unit you will need to demonstrate your knowledge and skills for each assessment objective for the unit. When you have completed three units as described above, you will be awarded a 'Certificate in iMedia', which has a points value on the National Qualifications Framework.

An important part of creating your work will be to explain why you have chosen to do something a particular way. This may be the equipment used or the techniques involved in creating and editing your work. Employment in the media industries are increasingly in need of multi-skilled people who can work in a number of software applications. This is where the iMedia qualification fits in – by developing a range of core skills that cover digital graphics, web authoring, animation, sound, video and computer games. The skills learned on the course will give you a solid foundation in each subject area and should be enjoyable, because the content is intended to be very practical. Your final assignment for assessment and submission to OCR will give you the opportunity to evidence your abilities in response to an identified client brief.

STRUCTURE OF THE QUALIFICATION

You will gain the core knowledge, skills and understanding for each subject unit as part of the recommended guided learning hours. These skills will be demonstrated through your independent completion of an assignment at the end of the allocated time. The assignment does not have a time limit for its completion, although it will be under supervised conditions.

At both Levels 1 and 2:

- There are 30 guided learning hours per subject unit.
- A Certificate in iMedia requires three units = 90 hours.
- A Diploma in iMedia requires five units = 150 hours.

As part of the knowledge, skills and understanding, this qualification aims to develop:

- Your ability to plan work within defined timescales
- Your ability to review work in terms of overall quality and fitness for purpose
- Your knowledge of a range of different software applications
- Your ability to manage information and data in suitable formats
- Your skills and knowledge in contexts directly relevant to employment situations
- Your skills to assist and encourage progression and further study

Subject units and relevant chapters

Level 1		
Unit	Title	Look at:
1	Exploring the digital world of media	Chapter 1
2	Introduction to web page production	Chapter 3
3	Creating an animated object	Chapter 4
4	Introduction to digital imaging	Chapter 2
5	Digital sound and video	Chapter 7
6	Interactive media presentations	Chapter 5
7	Design and test computer games	Chapter 8

Level 2		
Unit	Title	Look at:
1	Digital graphics	Chapter 2
2	Web authoring	Chapter 3
3	Digital animation	Chapter 4
4	Interactive multimedia concepts	Chapter 5
5	Digital sound	Chapter 6
6	Digital video	Chapter 7
7	2D game engines	Chapter 8
8	Game design	Chapter 9

Unit structure

In general terms, the content of each unit is split into four parts that cover the four categories of assessment objectives. These are:

- Exploration
- Planning
- Producing
- Reviewing

Exploration – of the equipment and technologies is covered in Part 1 of each chapter.

Planning – is covered in Part 2 of each chapter. There is also some general guidance on this aspect later in this Introduction.

Producing – is covered in Part 3 of each chapter. It describes the skills you will need using a range of suitable software and hardware to create the final work.

Reviewing – is covered in Part 4 of each chapter. There is also some general guidance on this aspect later in this Introduction.

So for example, assessment objectives (1a) and (1b) would be part of exploration and (2a), (2b) would be the planning etc. (these are based on the new specifications published in Spring 2008).

A detailed look at the actual assessment objectives for each unit of the qualification can be found on the CD-ROM with this book.

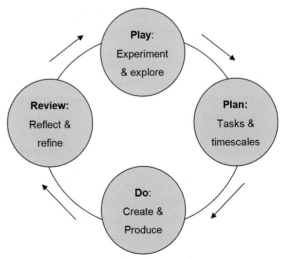

This four-stage process is shown as 'play – plan – do – review'. In this respect the concept of 'play' is to experiment and explore with the tools, techniques and equipment associated with the unit. This can be a valuable learning exercise and from this initial exploration, creative ideas may be generated. These ideas can then be used to plan what you are going to 'do' or produce in your final work. Note: in the diagram the review is shown feeding back into the exploration. However it could also feedback directly into either the plan or creation of the final work. The development of your work may follow a simple linear progression where the review is completed only at the end. This is fine but always consider that you can review any part of your work at any time as well.

ASSESSMENT

Once you have learned all the required parts of the unit, you will complete an assignment that will be used to assess your knowledge and skills of the subject. It will be set in a vocational context, which means that it will simulate what it would be like to be given a project by a client or employer in a work situation. This assessment will take the form of practical activities that are completed independently under supervised conditions. For example, in the digital graphics unit, you may be asked to obtain a series of photographs on a particular theme. These would be transferred to a computer and edited to create a final image that may combine several photographs with text.

The layout of the assignment will most likely be in four parts. These should follow the sequence of: explore solutions and possibilities – plan your work – produce your work – review what has been produced.

The place where you obtain information from will be called a *source* and you may use information from any relevant source to help with producing evidence for the assignment tasks. The information that is sourced could be a collection of images, sounds and animation files for example. These are referred to as the *assets* in your work. The *sources* and *assets* must be referenced in your work in order to recognise and credit the copyright on other people's work. Even so, there is a lot of information and assets that should not be reused in your own work because of copyright restrictions and your teacher will be able to advise you about this.

After completing the assignment, all evidence produced that supports the achievement of the assessment objectives for the unit and assignment is uploaded to an e-Portfolio. This activity may be completed by you or your teacher.

PLANNING YOUR WORK

For any assignment work, planning is an essential (and valuable!) part of the project work. As a minimum it will include a list of the activities you will need to complete it together with a description of the concept or a visualization/storyboard as appropriate to the chapter.

At first planning may not seem like a very exciting idea and you may just want to 'get on with it'. However, a little bit of planning and preparation can really improve the finished product.

For example, you may be attending a football match and need to take some photos. What happens if the batteries in the camera are almost flat because you didn't plan and prepare the equipment? The choice of camera will be important too – and dependant on where you will be taking the photos from. If standing at the back of the stalls, you are more likely to need a camera with a long telephoto lens setting. If working to a client brief, what do the final images need to show? Will you need close-up shots of players or a panoramic scene of the whole field?

Some of these questions will be answered after consultation with the client. They may give you a written specification or brief for what they want. If it is not very clear, you can ask to meet with them to discuss how the project will be completed and explain some of your ideas.

The style and type of planning method will be dependent on which chapter is being completed. For instance, a storyboard is a superb way of showing a series of different video shots such as for an interview and cut away to a scene. The framing and sequence that the frames are in will illustrate what video footage to actually record. The key word in this is that a *story* is being told, just like a comic book strip.

At Level 1 or 2, you could show the main assignment activities in a graphical format. This will also provide a good idea of the project timescale from start to finish.

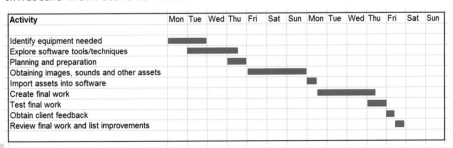

Activity	Mon	Tue	Wed	Thu	Fri	Sat	Sun	Mon	Tue	Wed	Thu	Fri	Sat	Sun
Identify equipment needed	■	■												
Explore software tools/techniques		■	■	■										
Planning and preparation				■										
Obtaining images, sounds and other assets					■	■								
Import assets into software								■						
Create final work								■	■	■	■			
Test final work											■			
Obtain client feedback												■		
Review final work and list improvements													■	

At Level 2 the planning process is more formal and you should use at least one of the planning techniques that are referred to in the OCR assignments. These ask you to use 'conceptualizsation, visualiszation and/or a storyboard as appropriate'.

For example, there are three approaches to the design of digital media products:

1. What the client wants
2. What the designer can do
3. What the user needs are (considering the age and ability of the actual users).

Questions that you could ask yourself when you have completed the initial design include:

1. Will it look good?
2. Will it work?
3. Will it do what you want it to do?
4. Is it what the client wants?

Conceptualization

This basically means anything that describes or shows what the basic idea is. In a game design, it would not necessarily mean showing what the game screen would look like. Instead, a concept drawing might show graphically what the game objective is, for example, get over the obstacles and find the treasure. Note here that a concept that is illustrated in a drawing is not the same as a visualization of what the game play will look like on the screen. In web design, the conceptualization could be an extension of a site map to describe or illustrate how site navigation works; a mock-up of one of the pages would be a visualization.

Visualization

If conceptualization describes the basic idea, then visualization shows what it will actually look like. In the game design example, this may be a mock-up of what the environment and terrain looks like when playing the game. That is, you are going to show people what they will see on the screen. In web design terms it is more

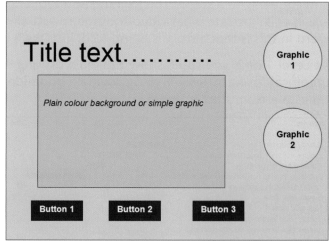

likely to be a layout of one of the web pages, possibly even including the colour schemes.

Storyboard

This is a series of sketches and is used to illustrate a sequence of events. Typically, you will need to create a storyboard for anything that uses moving images, such as animation or video clips.

Note the additional information and comments in the diagram.

Storyboard

Scene 1 (Title and intro)	Scene 2
Description of introductory scene *for example:* - short intro clip, 5 seconds max	Description of scene 2 *for example:* - what/where is the scene - who/what is in the scene - what happens next
Scene 3	Scene 4
Description of scene 3 *for example:* - what/where is the scene - who/what is in the scene - what happens next	Description of scene 4 *for example:* - dissolve to black - fade in closing credits

Mind maps/Spider diagrams

These are a good way to develop your ideas as you go along. They show the main areas for development and how the sequence of thoughts progresses.

The most common planning methods for the various chapters in this course would be:

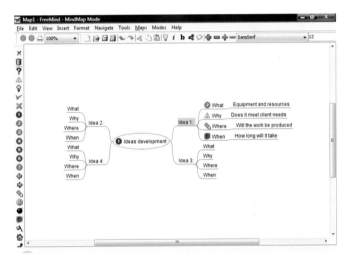

Chapter Unit	Conceptualize	Visualize	Storyboard
Digital world of media	✓		
Digital graphics	✓	✓	
Web authoring	✓	✓	
Digital animation	✓		✓
Interactive media	✓	✓	✓
Digital sound	✓		
Digital video	✓		✓
Computer games	✓	✓	
Game design	✓	✓	✓

REVIEWING YOUR WORK

You can learn as much from a review as from actually doing the work. This is because you can identify what has not worked very well so that it can be better next time. In this essential part of the assignment you will need to review how and why the final work is suitable for the original brief. So, if the assignment was to produce an image that could be printed at A4 – what does it look like? Are there any white borders; is the picture sharp; what is the dpi resolution? If it is a website – what does it look like when viewed in a web browser? If the navigation links between pages do not work, then it is not fit for purpose. How many websites have you visited and found a broken (non-working) link to the page you want? It can be quite frustrating. This is what you need to check for on your road to becoming a digital media pro.

List of assets used with sources

A file for this table can be found on the CD-ROM supplied with this book. It is in both Microsoft Word® and Adobe PDF file formats. You can complete this (or an equivalent) and submit it with your work – as well as use it in future projects.

Asset	Filename	Sourced from	Copyright status
e.g. photo	city_scene.jpg	website name	© website owner

Note: Most information sourced from Wikipedia is subject to the GNU public licence. When information is used, you will need to quote the source and the fact that it is covered by the GNU licence. Check the individual page permissions and copyright status each time you want to use anything.

The process of reviewing is about asking questions of the finished work as much as anything else. Sometimes it is difficult to be impartial when looking at your own work so ask other people to help with this. Invite some *constructive* comments and think about these when you receive them.

Below is a list of general questions that could be asked. Note that this is not a comprehensive list and some questions are specific to a particular chapter. However, these questions are a good starting point.

1. Does the final work satisfy what is asked for in the original brief?
2. What is the overall quality like?
3. Is the final work fit for purpose?
4. What has worked well – what is the best part?
5. What part of producing the work went better than expected?
6. What did not work well – which is the worst part?
7. What part of the final work could be better?
8. Where improvements could be made, how could these be achieved? (For example better source images/graphics/sounds vs. different editing and processing techniques.)
9. Does the navigation work? (For example, for websites and interactive multimedia presentations.)

This might look like a long list but you don't need to ask and write about every single question. Whatever questions are asked in the review, they must be relevant to the subject of the chapter, whether it is graphics, websites, animation, multimedia, sounds, video or games, and so on.

Specific information and guidance on how to review your work in the individual chapters is included at the end of each subject chapter. These general principles and ideas can then be adapted as required.

Digital World of Media

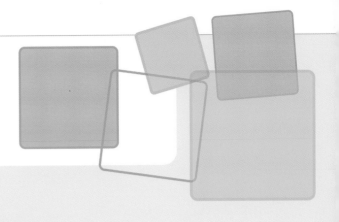

The aim of this unit is to explore the world of digital media and technology, which is now part of everyday life for most people. Some of the most commonly used technologies include computers, mobile phones and the World Wide Web. You will learn about the range of devices and capabilities of both digital technologies and the Internet. This includes a review of the benefits and potential risks and disadvantages of using the Internet. One of the aims is to make sure that you protect yourself and not disclose information that could put you at risk. Of course, there is a lot of fun to be had in the digital world as well! Let's start by looking at digital technology devices.

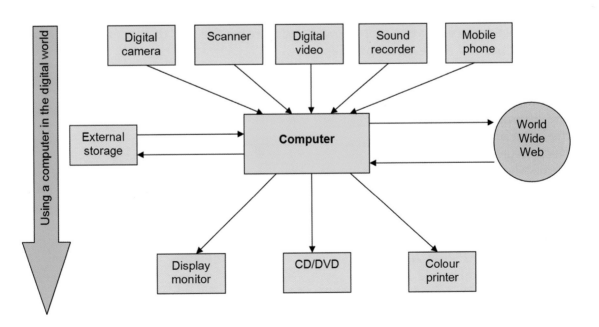

Capturing/recording sounds, images and video

Using a computer in the digital world

Digital camera · Scanner · Digital video · Sound recorder · Mobile phone · External storage · Computer · World Wide Web · Display monitor · CD/DVD · Colour printer

PART 1: EXPLORING THE DIGITAL WORLD

Digital technology devices

Computers

PC: A general term for either a desktop or laptop 'personal computer' that is used by a single person at any one time. The term is commonly associated with an IBM compatible computer system running a Microsoft Windows® operating system, although it can be thought of as any personal computer.

Key specifications

Processor

The CPU (central processing unit) is the brain of the computer and it is one of the main components that affects overall performance. Higher-speed processors use more power and increase the cost of the computer but will make tasks speedier.

Hard disk

This stores the operating system and software applications (once the latter are installed). Data files, documents and other media files are saved to the hard disk so that they can be used and edited using the computer software. Typical sizes for a hard disk are between 60GB (gigabytes) and 250GB. A large number of digital media files

(e.g. photographs, sound or video) will need disk sizes at the higher end of this range. SATA drives are faster than IDE to read/write information, which improves overall computer performance.

Memory

This is temporary storage used by the computer when it is switched on. Computer performance (speed) can be improved by adding more memory, especially if large video files are being edited or more than one software application is open at the same time.

Display

Display refers to screen size and technology. Older desktop PCs may have television-style CRT monitors (cathode ray tubes). Laptops have LCD screens in a typical range of 14.1, 15.4 and 17-inch sizes. Widescreen displays are more popular, especially if used to watch movies. Screen resolution refers to how many pixels (dots) of information are displayed, anything from 1024 × 768 to 1680 × 1050 are popular. The larger resolutions are found on the bigger screen sizes.

Media connections

These include USB ports for connections to printers, scanners, cameras and other devices. Some computers have media slots for memory cards used in digital cameras, for example, compact flash, SD, xD and memory stick. If using with digital video cameras (MiniDV), a FireWire port will be needed. These are built into some laptops and can be added to a desktop using a plug-in card.

Wireless connectivity

This is built into most laptops and added to a desktop using a plug-in card. The main use is to allow wireless connections to a router for access to the Internet. The Wi-Fi standard is also known as IEEE 802.11b/g.

Operating system

The main Microsoft systems for PCs are Windows® XP (Home and Pro versions) and Windows® Vista (versions for home and business users).

Apple Mac

An alternative to a Microsoft Windows®-based PC, they are popular with professionals working in the creative industries such as desktop publishing, graphic design, sound and video. Models include the PowerMac G4, G5 and iMac desktop computers together with MacBooks, which are portable notebook versions.

Main differences between an Apple Mac and a PC specification

Apple computers are now using Intel Pentium® Core 2 Duo processors for better software compatibility with PCs. They use 'Airport' cards for wireless connectivity and are usually fitted with both USB and FireWire. The operating system is Unix-based OSX 10.4 Tiger® or 10.5 Leopard®.

Media and other technology devices

PDA

This is a Personal Digital Assistant and may run a Microsoft Windows® CE operating system, which is a cut down version of the complete operating system for use on portable devices. A PDA provides popular utilities such as diary, calculator, notepad and address book. Depending on the model, it may have other features such as mobile phone, messaging, GPS (global positioning system), navigation, camera and Microsoft Office®-style software applications. PDAs can usually be synchronized with data on a computer so that documents and diary appointments are updated on both.

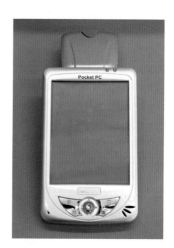

Mobile phone

Mobile phones are now established as a standard accessory device, and are now enhanced through features such as cameras, games, email, web browsing and other utilities. 3G stands for 'third generation', which provides high-speed connectivity.

MP3 player

A small and portable device for the playback of music. The individual tracks are stored in the mp3 audio file format, which can be downloaded to/from a computer. A file may have a filename such as 'track1.mp3'. A player will have a specified flash memory storage capacity such as 1GB, 4GB, 16GB, and so on. Higher capacity players can store potentially hundreds or even

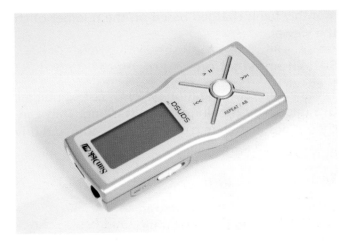

thousands of music tracks. MP3 players are made by a wide range of manufacturers such as Sony, Sandisk, Creative Zen, Samsung and Philips.

MP4 player

This is a small portable device for the playback of video clips and movies. A small display screen of typically 50–100mm (2–4 inches) is combined with audio playback. Video clips can be downloaded from the Internet and copied to the player using a computer. The Apple iPod nano and classic are popular examples of this type of player.

Games consoles

These can be portable devices such as the Sony PSP or Nintendo DS. Alternative full-sized platforms that connect to a television include the Microsoft Xbox, Sony Playstation and Nintendo Wii. Some of these consoles also provide additional connectivity for Wi-Fi networks and can be used to playback various media formats such as mp3, mp4, CD/DVD, Blu-Ray and HD-DVD discs.

Digital television

This is replacing analogue television broadcasting and provides more channels in addition to interactivity features. Freeview channels are free to air and do not incur any additional costs to receive the signals. Cable and satellite are also forms of digital television but a monthly fee is charged based on the number of channels chosen by the viewer.

Satellite navigation

These are in-car navigation systems that combine built-in maps with GPS (global positioning system) tracking. They can be setup with a chosen destination (e.g. using a postcode) and driving instructions are displayed in real time.

Sound recording

Voice memos, interviews, music and background sounds can be recorded using a range of devices, for example portable digital recorders, dictation machines, video cameras (with built-in microphones), computers, mobile phones, PDAs, and so on.

Imaging devices

Cameras

Still images can be captured using one of several types of digital camera, for example SLR (single lens reflex), compact or mobile phone. Photographs are stored on flash memory cards and transferred to a computer for storage.

Alternatively, the photographs can be printed at a photographic store (or even some supermarkets) without having to use a computer.

Video

Moving images can be recorded using most digital compact cameras, dedicated video cameras and some mobile phones. Depending on the camera being used, the video may be stored on a tape, hard disk, DVD or electronic memory.

It is either transferred or 'captured' to the computer system for editing purposes.

Scanners

Scanners are connected to a computer using a USB connection. The most popular types are A4 flatbed, which can be used to scan text, images and small objects. Some have special adaptors for scanning slides (transparencies) and negatives. These need light that is transmitted through the slide rather than reflected off the surface.

Printers

Inkjet

Inkjet printers are used in the home and business, for printing a range of letters, graphical documents and photographs. They use at least four colours: C-M-Y-K (cyan, magenta, yellow and key, or black). Photographic quality printers will have six or more colours, adding light cyan (LC) and light magenta (LM). Some printers have two different blacks to produce a better range of contrast.

Multi-function devices combine a scanner and printer, which also enable it to be used as a copier. Some have memory card slots to enable printing of photographs directly from the memory card of a digital camera. This means that a computer is not needed to produce prints, because everything is controlled from a panel and LCD on the printer.

Laser

Laser printers are used in businesses as fast, high-volume letter and document printers. Many only have a black toner cartridge and cannot produce colour prints. Recently, colour laser printers have become more widely available and cost effective, although they do not have the same photo-quality print capability of inkjet printers.

Photo printers

These are dedicated printers for 100 × 150mm (6 × 4 inch) photo-quality prints. They can be connected directly to a camera using a PictBridge interface and cable. Alternatively, they may also have memory card readers built in to enable printing directly from the card using the printer controls and LCD display.

Storage devices

Hard disks

These are mechanical devices with large storage capacities. Computers have at least one internal hard disk for the operating system and installation of software applications. External hard disks provide very useful additional storage, which can also be used for making a backup copy of important data, photographs and other files.

CD/DVD/Blu-Ray discs

These are all different types of optical disc storage. They are long lasting when stored correctly and very useful for backing up important files. Storage capacities are increasing with new technologies such as Blu-Ray and HD-DVD.

Type of disc	Storage capacity (single-sided)
CD	700MB
DVD	4.7GB
HD-DVD	15GB
Blu-Ray	25GB

LightScribe discs are a special type of DVD that have a surface coating that can be etched using the laser of the DVD drive. This is a long-lasting method of labelling discs rather than using adhesive labels or inkjet printable surfaces. After the data has been

recorded to the disc, it is turned upside down in the drive to enable the laser to write on the surface.

Memory stick/flash drive

These are electronic storage media that do not lose information when power is removed. The technology used is flash memory and it is packaged in a range of different formats for digital cameras and portable-storage pen drives. Storage capacity is increasing as technology improves, from budget-priced 1GB models to 16GB models or more.

Software applications

There are two types of software found on computers: system software and application software.

System software

This is the operating system that is supplied with the computer, for example, Windows® XP, Vista or Mac OSX Tiger or Leopard. The operating system will boot the computer, provide file and folder management and the desktop graphical user interface.

Application software

Any programs that are installed for editing photographs, writing letters, recording sound or playing games will be application software. These are purchased and installed either from CD/DVD or possibly downloaded from the Internet.

All software is covered by a licence that describes the terms and conditions of its use and installation. The conditions are set by the developer or publisher of the software. Again there are two main types of software licence: proprietary and open source.

Proprietary

The software developer maintains ownership and all copyright on the software that is being used or installed. The user must agree to the licence terms during installation. In effect, the end user who has purchased the software has only purchased a licence to *use* the software but does not actually own it. The terms and conditions often state that a single copy may be installed. Sometimes a second copy may be installed on a different computer by the purchaser as long as both computers are not used at the same time. Examples of proprietary software include Microsoft Windows® operating systems and Adobe applications.

Open source

The software developer or publisher 'openly' passes on ownership of the software to the end user. There is a growing range of open source software available that can be freely downloaded and installed on as many computer systems as needed. There is no licence fee and the code can even be redeveloped by the end user as long as any new version is distributed under the same licence terms. Examples of open source software are Linux-based operating systems, Open Office, The Gimp (for graphics editing) and Audacity (for sound editing).

Online Software

Some software is now being made available by accessing the Web. To use the applications, it is not necessary to download or install the software on the computer system. A fee is paid on a monthly or yearly basis to access the website and software applications.

The digital world and the Internet

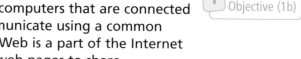

The Internet is a very large network of computers that are connected all over the world. The computers communicate using a common protocol called TCP/IP. The World Wide Web is a part of the Internet that uses text, images and graphics on web pages to share information. So the Internet is used to connect to other computers and information is retrieved from the Web.

In order to view information on the Web, a web browser must be used. This is a software application on a computer system connected to the Internet and it is used to 'browse' or 'surf' between websites. Netscape was the first browser to be widely used although it is no longer available or supported. Popular current browsers are:

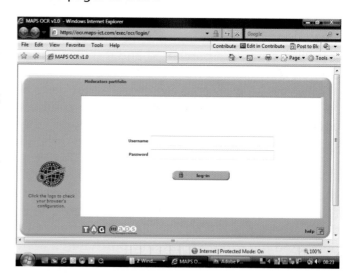

- Microsoft Internet Explorer® (proprietary to Microsoft)
- Mozilla FireFox (open source)
- Opera (open source)
- Apple Safari® (proprietary to Apple)

Wired connections to the Internet

Dial-up

Before broadband connections, computers would use a modem on a telephone line to dial in to an Internet Service Provider (ISP). Typical speeds were relatively slow at 56kbps, which is enough for the display of text pages but not so good for high-resolution images, video, rich media and downloading.

Broadband

Broadband is a general description for a fast connection to the Internet. Download speeds from 512kbps through to 30Mbps or more can be considered to be broadband connections.

Wireless and mobile network connections to the Internet

Mobile Web

Mobile Web is a recent development with typically 1.8Mbps or higher connection speed using HSDPA (High Speed Downlink Packet Access). Wireless broadband modems can be connected to a computer using a USB port. If an HSDPA signal is not available in your location, it is likely that you will still have a slower GPRS connection. UK coverage for mobile broadband will improve quickly as the demand increases.

Wi-Fi Router

GPRS

GPRS (General Packet Radio Service) has connection speeds of between 56 and 114kbps. EDGE GPRS provides up to 236kbps. It is used for data transfer on mobile phone networks, such as surfing the Web using a WAP browser.

HSDPA Modem

Wi-Fi

Wi-Fi stands for Wireless Fidelity. This is a term used to describe radio connections between a computer and a modem or router that is usually connected to the Internet. It allows web browsing without wires and is also available in a growing number of wireless hotspots in the UK. A single account with The Cloud, Boingo or JiWire gives access to any wireless hotspot for a monthly fee. Many portable devices such as the Apple iPhone and some portable games consoles can be used with Wi-Fi.

Bluetooth

This is another form of wireless connection designed for close-range communications, such as between a mobile phone and computer. It is typically used for exchanging information.

Web construction – addressing and domains

In the same way that every house in the country has an address, every computer on the Internet has an IP (Internet Protocol) address. Websites are hosted using domain names, which are easier to remember than IP addresses. For example, the OCR website has a domain name of: http://www.ocr.org.uk.

The 'http' refers to hypertext transfer protocol, which describes the way in which information can be communicated. A domain name server (DNS) is used to translate the domain name into the IP address of the computer where the website is hosted. If you know the IP address of a host computer, this can also be typed into a browser address field, for example http://81.144.255.114.

Search engines

The World Wide Web holds a very large amount of information. Unless you know the domain name of the website you need, the next step is to use a search engine to filter results based on key words. These search engines have already indexed a large number of websites and pages. When you complete a search, the search engine looks in its own database to list the pages that may be

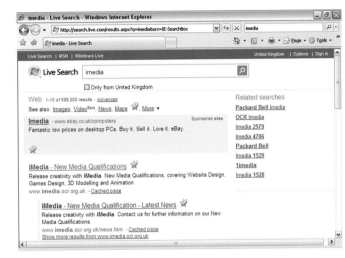

suitable and the process is very quick. Popular search engines include Google, Yahoo, Alta Vista and Ask in addition to those built into a web browser such as Microsoft Internet Explorer®.

Advanced searches

With advanced searches, you can specify more details of what should be listed in the search results. In Google's advanced search options, you can find results that:

- have **all** of the words
- have the **exact** phrase
- have at least **one** of the words
- does **not** have the words

A selection of 'operators' can also be added to a search string. The main ones are '+' and 'OR'. Examples would be:

- Mobile+Broadband
- Printers OR Printing

Benefits

A good search engine will speed up the process of finding the information that you need. The relevance of the results listed will depend on the information or 'search strings' that you enter. Sometimes just rewording what you are looking for can give a much better set of results.

PRACTICE EXERCISE

Research digital technology devices

1. Make a list of digital technology devices used by people around you.
2. Use an Internet search engine to find out what the devices can do. Look for the main features, capabilities and specifications.
3. Check to see whether people are using the devices to their full potential.
4. List some of the extra things that the devices could be used for and talk to the owners about them.

Downloads

Benefits

A file that has been downloaded becomes a local copy of the information that is stored for later use. This means the information will be accessible without needing to reconnect to the Internet.

Issues

Issues include copyright permissions, file sizes and locations. One of the problems with downloading from the Internet is the possibility of breaking copyright laws. Text documents, images, photographs, videos or music placed on the Internet are protected in the same way as any other artistic or creative works. It is the author of the work who holds the copyright unless it has been transferred to somebody else. Just because something is in the public domain (in this case, the Internet) this does NOT mean that it is copyright free. If you download or use anything from the Internet (or anywhere else for that matter), check to see if it is declared copyright free before using it in any of your own work – *especially* if you are going to publish it back into the public domain.

Online shopping and payment security

Personal data

When online shopping, you will need to enter your personal details such as name, address, telephone and payment information. Most sites will ask you to register first so that they can track your account orders. Registration involves creating a username and password, which you then use to login to your personal account each time you visit the site. Registration usually asks for home address and email contact information.

Payment security

Look for https:// as the prefix in the domain URL (as opposed to http://). The 's' denotes that the site is hosted on a secure or encrypted server. The web browser should also display a padlock icon either at the top or bottom of the window. If the padlock is closed, this confirms that a secure connection has been established and all the information transferred will be encrypted.

Types of shopping

Retail

There are a large number of businesses selling their goods on the Internet. Items for purchase are placed in a shopping cart and the buyer proceeds to a checkout. The buyer then enters the payment information, usually by credit or debit card, and confirms the delivery address. One well-known example is Amazon, which was one of the first of the dot.com retailers to become very successful through Internet sales.

Bid-up auction

In bid-up auctions, items are listed for sale by auction to the highest bidder. There is often a time limit or an end time when bidding will finish, such as the system used by eBay. At the end of the listing, the item is sold to the highest bidder as long as it has met any quoted reserve price.

Reverse auction

In this situation the role of the buyer and seller are reversed. Although it is still described as an auction, the buyer states what they want and potential sellers place bids (or offers) for what they are prepared to sell at.

Check the terms and conditions for any restrictions, such as minimum age, and check any web page that asks you for payment card information to make sure that it is secure.

Communications

Messenger services and email

Instant messenger services enable two or more people to 'talk' to each other online using the keyboard and computer screen. The messaging service is real time so that a message typed in is seen immediately on the receiver's screen. The only requirement is that both people are online at the same time. A new contact can be created just by knowing an email address.

Email is 'electronic mail' that is sent immediately to an email address that has been created already. It is not necessary that two people are online at the same time as the message will be retrieved when the receiver is next online and 'checks' for email. Nearly all retailers and suppliers have contact email addresses and they will ask for yours when you place orders or register to use their website.

Benefits

Both messenger services and emails are sent almost instantly. Hence it is possible to have written contact with somebody on the other side of the world as if they were next door. Messenger chat rooms are private and can only be read by the two individuals (or as many as have been invited). Even if you are online, you can change your status to show that you are 'busy' or even 'offline'. This enables you to work on the computer without any of your contacts knowing you are online, if you wish to.

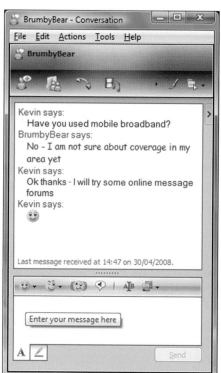

Drawbacks

Messages can only be received when people are online and connected to the Internet. You cannot know when anybody will next connect to download their email messages.

Security

Standard email is not secure or encrypted. The contents could be seen by anybody. You should never send confidential information such as bank account numbers or passwords in an email or using instant messenger services. For more information on your online security, have a look at http://www.thinkuknow.co.uk. This covers a wide range of online security issues such as instant messaging, mobiles, blogs, chat rooms, file sharing and cyber bullying.

Sharing

Messenger chat can also be shared between more than two people. Just invite as many others as you like who are shown in your contact list.

Language

The use of texting on mobile phones and instant messaging has created its own language. The following are some abbreviations for commonly used phrases and these can be useful to save time and the number of characters (letters) in messages:

- 2nite – tonight
- b4n – bye for now
- gr8 – great
- lol – laugh out loud
- rotfl – roll on the floor laughing
- thx – thanks

Discussion forums/Chat rooms

Purpose

The purpose of discussion forums and chat rooms is to discuss issues on a particular subject among like-minded people. There are specialist websites as well as Yahoo user groups covering a broad range of subjects. Browse for a forum with a subject or topic of interest and then join in.

Security

Personal security – never give out personal information such as home address, school or where you go. Never trust a stranger you have met in a chat room, even if they appear to be genuine.

Advantages

These forums can be good sources of information, and are often used by very knowledgeable people.

Disadvantages

People might not be who they say they are or claim to be. It is just as easy for somebody to lie about themselves in an online community as it is in real life. Information quoted may be incorrect or unreliable so best to double check somewhere else if possible. Anything said in a chat room can be read by everybody who has signed up to the forum – there is no private or confidential contact.

Blogs/social networking/Wikis

Blogs

A 'blog' is abbreviated from 'weB logs' and is a personal online journal or diary. It consists of a personal log of events, thoughts, feelings, news and experiences. The site may be set up to be private among selected friends or completely open to the public. Care must be taken about the information posted on public blog sites for your own security. Websites that provide blogging services include www.blogger.com and www.thoughts.com.

Social networking

Social networking sites are similar to blogs, but are more like personal websites that are only accessible to selected contacts unless opened up to the public domain. Examples include Microsoft Windows® Live Space, Facebook®, Bebo® and MySpace®. Typical content includes a personal profile, photos and blogs.

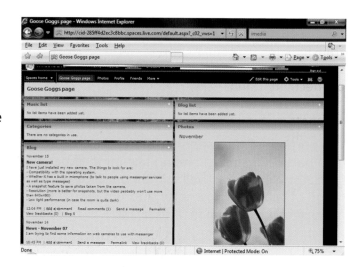

Wiki

This is a website that allows users to create, edit and modify the page content. Wikipedia is a good example and is one of the largest online encyclopaedias. All of the information and articles are submitted freely by users of the website http://www.wikipedia.org.

VLE

A 'virtual learning environment' is a web-based resource to provide information and guidance on coursework and is easy to update in a similar way to a wiki. It is used by both teachers and learners. Many schools, colleges and other training centres use VLEs, many of which are developed using open source applications such as Moodle.

Skype and VoIP

Skype uses Voice over Internet Protocol (VoIP) to make free telephone calls between people with Skype accounts. Calls to landline and mobile phones can also be made at cheap rates. Once accounts are created, users connect a Skype-compatible telephone to a USB port on the computer. Contact is made using the Internet connections of both people.

Mobile technology

Mobile phone technology covers hardware devices, networks, connectivity and services. In addition to voice calls, network operators also provide a range of data information transfers either by GPRS or mobile broadband (HSDPA). First-generation phones were based on voice calling. Second generation (2G) uses higher speed data transfers such as GPRS. Third-generation (3G) phones use even higher data transfer speeds. Not all phones support wireless broadband connectivity using 3G. An alternative is Wi-Fi access at hotspots such as airports, hotels and pubs. Some telephones such as the original Apple iPhone incorporated Wi-Fi connectivity for faster web browsing and email services.

Options

There is a wide choice of mobile phones from manufacturers such as Apple, LG, Motorola, Nokia, Samsung and Sony Ericsson.

These can be connected to one of the mobile network providers, which include:

- O2
- Vodafone
- Three
- Orange
- T-Mobile

Tariffs determine the amount paid for the services received. They vary depending on the number of included minutes and SMS text messages. Monthly contracts are available, which are paid by direct debit from the bank. Alternatively, pay-as-you-go accounts enable users to pre-pay their usage of the mobile network. Top-ups can be purchased at many high street stores.

Benefits

Mobile technology is very portable and telephones now combine a wide range of devices such as:

- telephone
- address books
- text and multimedia messaging
- digital camera (stills and video)
- sound recording
- web browser
- email
- diary
- alarms
- calculator
- games

Although these are sold as mobile phones, it would be better to describe some of them as multifunction devices that also include a telephone! A BlackBerry is a special type of mobile device that has a complete QWERTY keyboard (i.e. with a key for every letter of the alphabet). This is used with text messages and email. The full keyboard layout makes it much easier and quicker to type long messages, when compared to the ten number keys on a standard phone, which have three or four letters per key.

Drawbacks

The cost of calls, multimedia messages and web access can easily add up to a fair amount of money each month. Signal coverage is not 100 per cent throughout the country and high-speed data connectivity, such as with mobile broadband, is not yet fully established.

PART 2: PLANNING RESEARCH AND OBTAINING INFORMATION

1 Objective (2a)

Definitions of primary and secondary sources of information

Primary sources

This is where you obtain information directly from the original source. The information is obtained 'first hand' either by direct contact or discussion with somebody who has authored/created the original work, for example by telephone or face-to-face conversation. Hence the information has not already been interpreted by somebody else, which should mean that it is more reliable and factually correct.

Secondary sources

This is where information is received 'second hand'. One example would be where the information is obtained through a third party or otherwise passed on as an opinion of what somebody told a friend of a friend who talked to somebody else in a chat room. In other words, secondary sources are usually less reliable than primary sources because they are based on one or more people putting their own interpretation on the information. Some examples would be books, magazines, forums, videos and any conversation with somebody who is repeating what they have heard.

In your work you will need to identify what information has been obtained from primary sources and what information has been obtained from secondary sources. You will need to use both sources of information in your final assignment.

Electronic sources of information

The Internet is a huge source of information with billions of web pages. Search engines can be used to sort through this as seen earlier in this chapter. The format of electronic or digital information covers a wide range of text, graphics, moving images, video and sounds. Subject to copyright restrictions, you may be able to obtain information from websites such as:

- manufacturers' websites
- retail/distributors' websites
- blogs
- wikis
- discussion forums
- chat rooms

The format of the electronic information may be:

- text
- graphics and images, for example .jpg, .gif, .png
- video, for example QuickTime, .mov, .avi
- sounds, for example .mp3
- PDF files (portable document format)
- podcasts

You may be able to obtain some of this information by download as well as by copying and pasting information from web pages.

You will need to acknowledge all your information sources. This can be quite easily done in a table of information, an example of which is included on the resource CD. Highlight any information or sources that have copyright restrictions. When using an online encyclopaedia such as Wikipedia, check to see if the information is covered by the GNU (General Public Licence). If it is, you can use the information as long as you quote the licence in your work.

CD/DVD sources of information

Encyclopaedias such as Britannica or Microsoft Encarta® are available on CD and DVD. Library images and clip art can be found on photo discs, some of which are royalty free and possibly even copyright free.

Paper-based sources of information

These include books, magazines, journals and newspapers. Try your local library and make notes of any useful information. Some information can be scanned, copied or photographed but once again check the permissions before using it in any of your work. Specialist monthly magazines such as those on computer games and mobile technology will keep you up to date on current and new trends.

PART 3: EVIDENCING RESEARCH IN A MEDIA FORMAT

After you have researched a subject, it will need to be reported in some type of media format. Your work can be produced in a number of ways using a wide range of software. It could be in the form of a presentation, publication or social networking site on the Web. More information on the software applications in the following sections can be found in later chapters of this book.

1 Objective (3a)

Presentation

Software applications such as Microsoft PowerPoint®, Microsoft Publisher®, Adobe Flash® or Apple Keynote® could be used to create this. Any of these formats can easily support a combination of text and graphics.

Microsoft Powerpoint®

Audio/Video

Using a video or web camera, record yourself talking about the research that you have completed and the conclusions you have come to. You may need to use some sort of video editing software to save the video in a suitable file format and size. Examples of this would include Windows Movie Maker®, Adobe Premiere Elements® and Apple iMovie®.

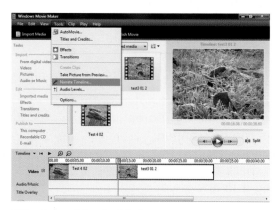

Windows Movie Maker

Web pages

You have a choice of creating a website using web authoring software or building a social networking site such as those on Microsoft Windows® Live Space, Facebook, Bebo and MySpace. If the latter are used, you will need to use screen captures to show the content rather than just providing a web link in your final work. Authoring of websites can be completed using Adobe Dreamweaver® or Microsoft FrontPage® (Expression Web®).

Multimedia

Any method of combining text and graphics with sound and video produces a multimedia product. This may be an extension of a website or presentation, using one or more of the software applications already mentioned.

Publication/report

This could be a document with text, images and screen captures. Software applications that could be used include Microsoft Word®, Microsoft Publisher® or Apple Pages®.

Always save your files using a suitable name that describes the content. If using specialized software, you may also need to export the work into a standard format that can be viewed on any computer system. For example, if using Adobe Flash, export the work in .swf format for viewing with Flash Player in a web browser.

PRACTICE EXERCISE

Explore software choices for creating work

1. Review what software is installed on your computer system.
2. List what software applications could be used to create your final work in a media format.
3. Identify what media formats are supported and how these are inserted into the software application, for example, .jpg images, .mov video and .mp3 sound.
4. Review what format will be needed to save your final work and check what will be needed to view this on a different computer system.

PART 4: REVIEW YOUR COMPLETED WORK

When you have finished your work, you will need to think about it in terms of the strengths, weaknesses and any areas for further improvement. You may want to obtain some constructive comments from friends and the client in order to answer these questions. You could also refer to the general comments in the section on Planning and Review in the Introduction.

1 Objective (4a)

When reviewing your work, ask yourself the following questions:

1. Does the final work show what the client brief actually asked for?
2. Is the media file size suitable? In other words, make sure it is not too large.
3. Is the media file format suitable? For example, can it be viewed on a different computer system?
4. Is the final work easy to read and pleasing to look at? If it is, then you could say it was a strength, if not it could be a weakness. Be fair and honest with yourself and see if others agree with you.
5. What improvements could be made? For example, you could obtain different information or use different software to create your final work.

SUMMARY

The purpose of this unit is to learn more about the digital world and keep up to date with recent developments. Hopefully you will have explored the use of some different technologies and be more aware of both the benefits and potential disadvantages. When downloading or copying information from the Web, always check whether there are any copyright restrictions on what you can do with it. If you create a piece of work, then you will hold copyright on it. Likewise, if somebody else has created something and put it on the Web, they still own the copyright unless they have specifically stated that it is 'open source' or covered by a public licence. Whenever publishing information about yourself on the Web, think carefully about whether it is safe to do so – especially when creating public profiles that are open for anybody to look at.

FINAL ASSIGNMENT

Once you have learned all the required parts of the unit you will complete an assignment that will be used to assess your knowledge and skills of the subject. It will be set in a vocational context, which means that it will simulate what it would be like to be given a project by a client or employer in a work situation. To start you should read the brief or scenario carefully to identify what is needed. A typical assignment may be in the following format (although these should not be used as templates for designing your own assignments – refer to the guidance documents on the OCR website for this purpose):

Brief:
You are a junior researcher for Tulipa Rossa, and have been asked to find out about communication methods used by people in the 16–19 age group. The owner has requested that your work is presented in a digital media format and must include examples of both primary and secondary research.
Task 1: In this task you will be asked to plan the development of your work. Use one or more of the planning methods described in the Introduction, identifying what you will need and how long it is likely to take.
Task 2: Here you may be asked to research and explore a range of

communication methods used by young people and gather sample images and other text information.

Task 3: In this task you will be asked to produce or create your work. This should demonstrate a range of skills using the hardware and software as appropriate for the media format chosen. Examples would be a multimedia presentation, web page, digital graphic/poster, video clip etc.

Task 4: In this task you should review your final work. This means thinking about things like overall quality, fitness for purpose and any areas for improvement. It is not just a summary of how you created the work – it should be a reflection by yourself (and others) on how suitable it is for use by the client described in the brief.

Note that essential parts of the assignment include the planning and reviewing of your work. It is important to be able to think about what you need to produce and what the final work should look like. Since the assignment is in a vocational context it will be important to check the suitability of what you have produced before submitting it to the client. The development of these skills will be a great benefit when you are asked to produce something in the real/commercial world of employment.

Digital Graphics/ Digital Imaging

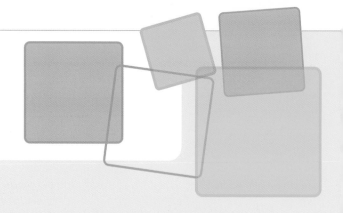

The aim of this unit is to develop the ability to use a digital camera to capture images that can be edited and saved in different formats. Some of the image editing software options are covered in this chapter, although you may also need to refer to the manuals for the software that you have available. The basic skills are common to most applications so you will soon learn how to adapt them.

Where, when and why do we use digital graphics?

1 Unit 4

2 Unit 1

Have a look around you – photographs and digital graphics surround us. Whether they are used on websites, magazines, poster boards or games, the market is enormous. Some areas where graphics are used would be:

- publishing (e.g. magazines, leaflets, newspapers, books, posters)
- advertising (print, web, video and other multimedia formats)
- websites (see Chapter 3 on Web authoring)
- presentations (see Chapter 5 on interactive media)
- CD-ROMs
- games (see Chapter 8 and 9 for game engines and game design).

PART 1: EXPLORING DIGITAL GRAPHICS AND IMAGES

For both Level 1 and Level 2, the aim is to develop skills in using a digital camera to take a series of photographs. These should be indoors and outdoors with a variety of different subjects. You will learn how to use the camera settings and controls to obtain good quality photographs. The composition of the photographs will also be an important part and you should be able to identify and use the basic rules of photography in your work. When you take any photographs, it is a good idea to use the LCD on the camera to play back the pictures taken. Check them for overall image quality by using the zoom controls in this mode. It will help you to identify if there is any movement or blurring in the picture.

 Objective (2a)

 Objective (1a)

PRACTICE EXERCISE

Research and review the use of digital graphics

1. Collect some images from a range of magazines and advertisements.
2. Identify what has been used in the images, e.g. multiple photographs and text.
3. Review the image quality, e.g. brightness, contrast, sharpness and composition.
4. List some key features or reasons why the images work (or not, as the case may be).

Bitmap/raster and vector graphics

There are two main types of graphics which have very different characteristics.

Bitmap/raster images

Bitmap/raster images are based on *pixels* and are produced by digital cameras or scanners. These pixels contain colour information as a mixture of red, green and blue. There is a limit to how far they can be enlarged or viewed at high magnification, because the image will become 'pixelated', that is, the eye can begin to see the individual pixel shape, colour and position. For use on a computer screen, you will need to use either 72dpi or 96dpi (dots per inch). You can check your monitor settings from [Microsoft Windows® XP] the control panel > Display > settings > advanced. For print use, you will ideally need 300dpi but acceptable results can be obtained from 200dpi upwards.

One of the potential disadvantages of bitmap graphics is that they do not scale well. If you open a bitmap image in an application such as Adobe PhotoShop® and begin to zoom in to a magnification larger than 100 per cent, you will notice that the image is broken down into small squares (keep zooming in and this will become even more apparent). Each of these little blocks is a pixel that contains only one colour. If you enlarge a bitmap image too far, you may notice that the image quality suffers from 'pixelation' because it is composed of these individual pixels or 'colour squares'.

Vector graphics

The other type of graphic is called a vector graphic, which is independent of resolution and maintains crisp edges when resized. These do not use pixels and the edges are very smooth even when resized (without any loss of graphical quality). This is because they are based on mathematical formulas that represent curves and lines. Vector graphics are typically shapes and text that are drawn using the shape, pen or text tools. Vector graphics can be converted to raster images for further editing as needed.

iMedia	iMedia
Bitmap or raster-based graphics at high magnification	Vector-based graphics at high magnification

Types and parts of digital cameras

There are many types of digital camera available, most of which share some similar parts and components. Some of the options are as follows:

1 Objective (2a)

2 Objective (1a)

Mobile phone camera

Generally these provide quite basic facilities for image capture. Check the resolution carefully for what is needed because many will be much lower than true digital cameras. However, they are very convenient to carry around even though they are difficult to hold steady for a sharp picture.

Compact camera

There is a wide choice of compact cameras from small pocket-sized to 'prosumer' (i.e. professional consumer) models that are almost the same size as a digital SLR. Most can also be used to record short, low-resolution video.

Digital SLR camera

SLR stands for 'single lens reflex' and allows the photographer to change the lens on the camera body (e.g. for wide angle, telephoto or macro lenses). They do not have a video mode but they are a popular choice for the serious amateur as well as the professional photographer.

Camcorder (with digital stills feature)

Many digital camcorders have a snapshot mode, which is for digital stills capture. As with mobile phones, check the resolution carefully and take a few test photos before using it for an assignment.

The choice of camera is not just about what is available – it is also about where and how the images will be used. For example, a mobile phone camera with 640 × 480 pixel resolution is not suitable if the final image is to be printed on the front cover of a magazine at A4 size. *This is one of the first steps to planning your work – choosing the right equipment for what you have been asked to produce.*

The parts of a camera

Camera body

This houses the main parts of the camera including the sensor, memory card, battery, image-processing electronics and operational controls.

Lens

This focuses the light from the subject onto the sensor. It has two main characteristics: the focal length and the aperture.

Focal length

Focal length affects how much of the picture is captured and many cameras are fitted with zoom lenses. This means that you can take wide-angle pictures or (by zooming in) take telephoto pictures. A typical compact camera may have a 3× zoom lens, which is usually equivalent to 35–105mm when compared to a traditional 35mm film camera. Use the best setting for the composition of the subject and the distance you are away from it.

Aperture

The aperture is one of the factors used to obtain the correct exposure and it works with the shutter speed. It can be thought of as the size of the hole in the lens for the light to pass through, which is controlled by the camera at the time the picture is taken.

Shutter

This is normally closed and opens for a short duration to allow light to pass through from the lens to the sensor. The duration the shutter is open is used in combination with the aperture to obtain the correct exposure, for example, a large hole in the lens will allow more light to pass through, so the shutter speed will be faster. Faster shutter speeds can 'freeze' movement whereas a slow speed increases the risk of camera shake. With a standard lens (focal length around 50mm), a safe speed should be 1/60th or faster, otherwise the pictures are likely to be blurred from camera shake (unless you use a tripod).

LCD and viewfinder

These are used to frame the picture, although the LCD (liquid crystal display) can be difficult to see on a bright day. The LCD is also used for the camera settings and menus.

Menu

The menu button will show several sections for picture taking and playback. Two of the basic settings to be familiar with are image size and quality. For instance, a 6 megapixel camera can be set to save 6, 3 or 1.5 megapixel images. The fewer pixels, the smaller the file on the memory card but it will not have as much detail at the lower end of this. Images with fewer pixels cannot be printed as large pictures because the detail is not recorded. On the other hand, image quality refers to the jpeg file format, with typical settings as fine, normal and basic. This controls the amount of compression that is applied to the file to keep the size down. More compression (the basic setting) will produce a smaller file. This will have a lower image quality, which may be noticeable at larger print sizes.

Flash

Often built into the camera, the flash provides a very short but bright flash of light to illuminate the subject. It has a limited range, so objects in the background may still be dark depending on how far away they are. When photographing people or animals, you may get 'red eye'. This happens when the flash is too close to the camera lens and the light reflects directly from the back of the subject's eye towards the camera. Fortunately there are tools in most photo-editing software applications to fix this.

Flash mode

Most digital cameras have a few different modes for the flash. Apart from auto (A) many cameras have a red-eye reduction mode. This fires a short flash before the main exposure to make the pupils of the subject's eyes smaller – which will reduce the amount of red eye in the final picture.

Memory card

This stores the photographs and is the electronic equivalent of film. There are various types and sizes of card. The larger the storage capacity of the card, the more photos can be saved on it. The type of card used varies depending on the manufacturer and the overall size of the camera, although they all use the same electronic technology.

Typical figures for 3, 6 and 12 megapixel cameras are:

No. of images	3MP JPG (normal)	6MP JPG (normal)	12MP JPG (normal)
256Mb card	300	150	75
1GB card	1200	600	300

The memory card can be changed easily in a digital camera. Fitting a higher capacity card of the same type will mean you can store more photographs on it.

The main types of memory card are:

- **Compact flash:** Usually found on larger camera bodies and digital SLR-type cameras.

- **SD card:** A small and popular card type, used in compact cameras and prosumer models.

- **xD card:** Originally developed by Fuji for use in their cameras as well as some Olympus models.

- **Memory stick:** Originally developed by Sony for use in their cameras, but also found in some others as well.

Batteries

Digital cameras use a lot of power. The two main parts needing power are the sensor and the main display (LCD). Hence, it is more economical to use rechargeable batteries than disposable ones. Digital cameras use one of two different types of rechargeable battery, depending on the manufacturer's design and the physical size of the camera:

- **NiMH or Nickel Metal Hydride:** A camera will usually have two or four AA size batteries. They are available in different capacities, quoted in terms of milliamp-hours (mAh). The higher the number of mAh the longer the battery will last before it must be recharged.

- **Li-Ion or Lithium Ion:** This is a more expensive technology but provides a large capacity in a small package. These batteries will be a special size and shape for the camera.

Camera accessories

In addition to the camera and any spare memory cards/batteries, there are a few other items of equipment that can be useful when taking your photographs:

- tripods to hold the camera steady and reduce camera shake
- external flash units when extra lighting is needed
- a range of different lenses for use with a digital SLR-type camera
- filters to put in front of the lens for special effects
- protective bags and cases to carry the camera and other accessories

---

PRACTICE EXERCISE

Explore your camera

1. Have a look at your camera to see what sort of battery is used – make sure that it is fully charged.
2. Check what type and size of memory card is fitted and how much free space there is.
3. Identify the shooting and playback modes.
4. Press the shutter button half way to see how it focuses on a subject.
5. Use the lens zoom controls to change the perspective of the picture.
6. Check to see what functions and features are provided in the menus.

Using a scanner

Objective (1a)

Scanners connect using a USB connection and are used to scan text documents, images and graphics. To use a scanner:

- Place the document face down on the glass plate.
- Slide the document up to the corner marked with an arrow to identify the origin or starting point of the scan.

- Either use the scanning software provided with the scanner installation, or import the scan directly into the graphics editing software. In Adobe PhotoShop this is found from the 'File' menu > 'Import'.

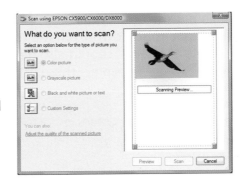

The WIA driver is used for basic scanning although more control can be found using the dedicated driver for the scanner. A scan resolution of 200dpi is adequate for most graphics although up to 300dpi can be used if the contents of the scan are likely to be enlarged.

Graphics tablets

These are an alternative to using a mouse and are popular with creative artists and designers. The use of a stylus pen on the tablet is similar to using a brush on paper. The thickness of a line can be changed by increasing or decreasing the pressure of the stylus on the tablet. They are ideal for drawing vector graphics and line art.

Basic rules of photography

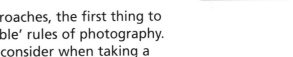

Although there are some recognised approaches, the first thing to remember is that there are no 'unbreakable' rules of photography. Think of them as more like guidelines to consider when taking a photograph. One of the most famous landscape photographers, Ansel Adams, once said '. . . there are no rules to good photographs, just good photographs'. However, some of the recognised basic rules are as follows:

Rule of thirds

This rule divides the image with imaginary grid lines at one-third increments both horizontally and vertically. Rather than put the horizon directly across the middle of the frame, try it either one-third down from the top or one-third up from the bottom. Points of interest should also be placed on the intersection of the lines where possible – these often make the photographic composition more pleasing to the eye. In the example shown, the horizon is one-third down from the top and the person is positioned on an intersection.

Use of lines

Lines are used to emphasise shape in a photograph and to draw the attention of the eye into the picture. They can be horizontal, vertical, diagonal or curved. Lines that start in one of the bottom corners can be very effective. In the example shown, the vapour trails start in the bottom left-hand corner and also the last plane is on an intersection of the one-third lines to balance the composition.

Use of frames

This is where shapes or objects are used to effectively put a border around the main subject. It focuses the eye and creates the boundary around the subject, which can be above, below or at either side (or a combination of these).

Perspective

This is about how different objects in the picture are seen in terms of their size and distance from the camera. A photograph of a building close up will have very little perspective (or depth) in the picture. A footpath that starts in the foreground and winds its way through a park into the distance has much more perspective. Wide-angle lenses generally give more perspective than telephoto lenses or settings.

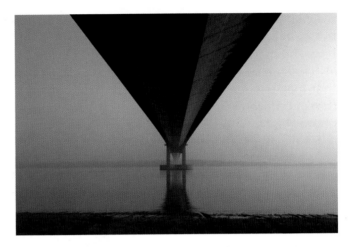

PART 2: PLANNING DIGITAL GRAPHICS PROJECTS

The choice of camera, settings and photographic composition will be an important part of the planning process. However, before planning the taking of photographs, you will still need to know what is required for the graphic project. This will be described in some sort of client brief or specification. Read this document carefully and think about how to satisfy the needs of the client using your own creative talents and ideas. Note down some ideas on how to complete both the photograph taking and image editing. Discuss all of your ideas with the client before taking any photographs.

 Objective (1a)

 Objective (2a)

Visualization diagrams and sketches are one of the best ways to plan your work for this subject. You will certainly need an equipment list and probably a concept of what will be created that you can show to your client. If you are developing initial ideas, try a spider diagram and see what you come up with. This is described in more detail in the section on Planning and Review in the Introduction if you are not sure about what needs to be included.

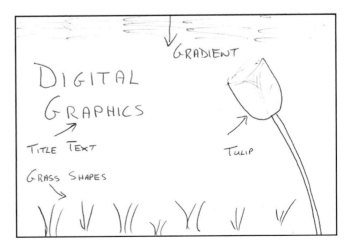

Visualisation Diagram

Of course you will need to document any use of copyrighted, trademarked or intellectual property. Keep records of all sources and permissions obtained for any material that is not your own. You may also need model and/or property releases for people and property that may be identified in your work. These releases are used to show that you have the right permissions to take and use the photographs.

Finally, think about how long the whole project will take. After your initial discussions with the client, they will want to know how long it will take to produce the work. Break this down into timescales for photograph taking and editing.

Creativity with digital graphics

At Levels 1 and 2 you should try to include two creative concepts in your work:

1. Rules of photography are the same as the rules of composition for digital graphics. Even if an original photograph does not use the rule of thirds, it may be possible to create a final graphic that does. Careful cropping and positioning of text, shapes and other elements can use any of the compositional guidelines described earlier in this chapter.

2. The colour schemes in your work should use colours that work well together. Complementary colours are opposite each other on the RGB (Red Green Blue) colour wheel. Note that artists use Red Blue Yellow as the colour wheel when mixing paints but this is different to mixing light. Using the colour wheel shown, yellow is the complement (opposite) of blue, hence a blue/yellow colour scheme works very well.

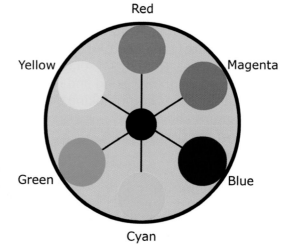

PART 3: CREATING AND EDITING DIGITAL IMAGES

PRACTICE EXERCISE

Taking photographs

1. Charge the batteries and clear the memory card of any old images.
2. Take a series of indoor and/or outdoor photos using different lens settings (wide and telephoto), with and without flash.
3. If working towards Level 2, think about the composition of the photographs and what rules of photography could be used to good effect. Take a series of photos of the same subject, some that use the rules and some that ignore them. Experiment with the camera settings in both automatic and manual modes, making a note of the camera settings such as shutter speed, ISO and white balance (WB).
4. As you take the photos, review them on the LCD screen. Use the zoom controls to magnify the image to check that is reasonably sharp (i.e. with no camera shake) and correctly exposed in the important areas.
5. Choose or create a suitable folder name on a computer system. Transfer the photos to this folder. Rename the images using suitable filenames, such as the date and time the photographs were taken, or use a description of the image content.

1 Objective (2a)

2 Objective (3a)

Saving digital images

2 Objective (3b)

The main file formats for use with digital graphics are:

.jpg This is the most common image file format, used in digital cameras and supported by web browsers. It gives a range of options for the amount of compression to reduce the file size, but at the expense of image quality. The format was originally developed by the Joint Photographic Experts group (JPEG).

.tiff Tagged Image File Format is very high quality with no loss of detail. TIFF files are used in print and desktop publishing applications.

.png Portable Network Graphics, an alternative to .jpg and intended as a replacement for .gif images without any licensing restrictions; .png is supported by the World Wide Web consortium although not all browsers display these correctly.

.gif Graphic Interchange Format, developed by CompuServe. This has a very limited range of 256 different colours, so is more suitable for graphics and logos than photographs. However it does support animation and transparency. It is commonly used on web pages even though officially the patent is still held by CompuServe.

Some additional file formats that you should know about for Level 2:

.bmp This is a bitmap file format developed by Microsoft for its graphics subsystem. It is usually uncompressed and can support a range of different colour depths.

.eps Encapsulated PostScript is used within high-quality desktop publishing applications.

.psd Adobe PhotoShop Document – this is the generic format used by Adobe in its graphics software. This format retains all the layers within the file structure for later changes or editing purposes. Adobe Creative Suite® CS3 upwards has support for layered PhotoShop or Illustrator® files in both Dreamweaver® and Flash® (which were originally Macromedia software). This means that the layers are also kept intact for editing purposes within these applications.

.pdf Portable Document Format – this is a widely used format for images, manuals, desktop publishing and other documents. A freely available reader (Adobe Acrobat®) means that these documents can easily be shared between computers and via the Internet.

.psp Paint Shop Pro document – this is the generic file format used by Corel in Paint Shop® software applications.

Transferring your photographs to a computer

There are two main options for transferring your photographs to a computer:

1. Use a USB cable to connect the camera to the computer (usually supplied with the camera). This can be fiddly if there is a mini USB connector on the camera, so be careful not to damage the socket. Remember the camera must be powered on for the transfer, so make sure that the batteries are charged before starting.

2. Use a card reader (remove the memory card from the camera and insert it into the reader).

Many multimedia computers have multimedia card readers built in so an external reader may not be required. Several inkjet printers also have card readers so check to see if you have one available that is already built in.

The image above shows a multipurpose card reader with a compact flash card and SD card in the reader.

Choosing a bitmap image-editing program

These are software applications that you can use to edit your photographs. There is a wide range of software available for this purpose, including the following:

- **Adobe PhotoShop:** An industry standard for use with photographs and graphic design. The range includes the Elements version together with professional-level versions such as 7.0 and Creative Suite (CS) variants. Adobe PhotoShop Elements is aimed at the home user, providing most of the commonly used features at a much lower cost.
- **Adobe Illustrator:** Also an industry standard, but more specific to graphics design and the use of vector graphics.
- **Adobe (Macromedia) Fireworks®:** Popular with those using graphics within web development and animation work.
- **Corel Paint Shop Pro:** A competitor for Adobe software that supports both bitmap and vector graphics, but only available for a Microsoft Windows®-based PC.
- **iPhoto®:** A basic image editing and photo management application that is part of the Apple Mac iLife® software. It can be used for Level 1 of this qualification but does not have the advanced editing tools necessary for Level 2.
- **Gimp:** A freely distributed open-source program for such tasks as photo retouching, image composition and image authoring. However it is also a very powerful image editing software application.
- **Adobe Lightroom®** is a professional software application for photographers, but only has a limited range of image editing tools so cannot meet the editing requirements at Level 2. It would however be ideal for Level 1 and especially those wanting to follow a career in digital photography (similar to Apple Aperture® in this respect). Inevitably though, there is often a need to use Adobe PhotoShop or an equivalent alongside these applications for more advanced and creative image editing.

Asset management and image processing

Many software applications will have a browser or organiser to manage the assets and images stored. These utilities provide previews of the images and often have a facility to 'tag' or 'rate' the images. A higher tag or rating is used for the best images. They can also be organised into 'stacks', which is a way of grouping images together that have a similar subject or content. In the illustration (right) taken from Adobe Bridge CS3®, the photographs have been given a star rating and the technical information about each image is shown in the lower right-hand panel.

1 Objective (3b)

2 Objective (3b)

Image processing and digital workflow

The basic editing techniques in many of the software applications are very similar so that skills learned in one application can often be quickly transferred into something else. The aim is to learn a basic workflow, which can be thought of as a standard sequence of editing techniques for every image. You can then use this workflow in whatever software application you have available.

1 Objective (3b)

An example of a basic workflow would be:

1. Review the image quality, exposure and sharpness.
2. Adjust the brightness/contrast or 'levels'. (Note that you only need to do *one* of these.)
3. Check and adjust the colour balance if necessary.
4. Crop to the required size, shape and resolution.
5. Save the image in a suitable format with a recognisable name.

These techniques are covered in more detail over the next few pages.

Using Adobe PhotoShop

1 Objective (3b)

2 Objective (3c)

1. Review the image quality

If the image quality is not good enough for what you need, you want to know immediately, otherwise you could be wasting your time with further editing. The best way to review the image quality is to use the zoom control to view the image at 100 per cent magnification. Check to see whether it is blurred or out of focus on the important subject areas. If the image quality is poor, close the file, open a different image or go out and take some more photographs – but this decision must always be based on the needs of the assignment you are working on. Remember: you cannot put quality or detail back into a

photograph using just a series of editing techniques. You will be able to rescue a poor photograph to some extent, but the results will be limited. A much better approach is to start with something good and move on from there.

2. Using the brightness/contrast adjustment sliders

One of the basic techniques as part of a workflow is to optimize the brightness and contrast. This makes sure that the full tonal range is used in the image, that is, the darkest (shadow) areas are a true black and the brightest (highlight) areas are true white. Without this optimization, a photograph can look 'washed out' or 'soft'. To do this, you could use the brightness/contrast adjustment sliders or levels histogram. The first thing to do is make sure you have a reasonable size of working image on the screen. You can do this by selecting the 'View' menu and then 'fit on screen'. There are automatic and manual controls for improving the image under the top level 'Enhance' menu (of Adobe PhotoShop Elements). These features are:

- Auto colour correction
- Auto levels
- Auto contrast

If the automatic controls do not work very well, manual adjustments can be made to the lighting, colour and brightness/contrast. These are also found under the 'Enhance' menu:

- Adjust lighting
- Adjust colour
- Adjust brightness/contrast

Depending on the version of Adobe PhotoShop being used and the level being studied, the tools/techniques used to achieve this important editing step can be summarised as follows:

	In PhotoShop CS	In PhotoShop Elements
Brightness/contrast adjustment (Level 1)	Image menu > Adjustments > Brightness/contrast	Enhance menu > Adjust brightness/contrast > Brightness/contrast
Levels histogram (Level 2)	Image menu > Adjustments > Levels	Enhance menu > Adjust brightness/contrast > Levels

Brightness/contrast sliders

This is a basic tool that allows you to make manual changes visually on the screen. Move the slider to the left or right until the best result is achieved.

Using the Levels histogram

The Levels histogram is a good way to check the overall exposure of the photograph and is a graphical display of how the picture is made up. It shows how the pixels in an image are distributed and whether they are mainly dark (at the left-hand side) or bright (towards the right-hand side). To make adjustments for the Levels, do the following:

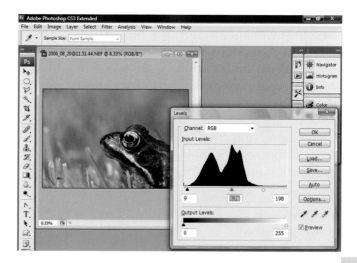

- Move the black point slider inwards from the left until it is at a point where the black shading on the histogram just begins.
- Move the white point slider from the right-hand side to a similar point.
- Move the mid point (gamma) slider to produce the best overall image on the screen.

The optimum positions for the black and white point sliders are shown in the above photograph (screen capture from Adobe PhotoShop CS3).

3. Changing and optimizing the colour balance

In Adobe PhotoShop Elements you can choose enhance – adjust colour – colour variations.

This allows you to add or subtract red/green/blue as needed to achieve the required result. If a photograph has a blue cast (such as a snow scene), this can be removed quite easily using this approach. The image can also be adjusted using hue and saturation. These are a set of sliders similar to the brightness and contrast. They enable you to change overall colour tone and colour saturation. You will notice that reducing the colour saturation to zero produces a black and white image.

The Levels histogram can also be used to correct the colour balance:

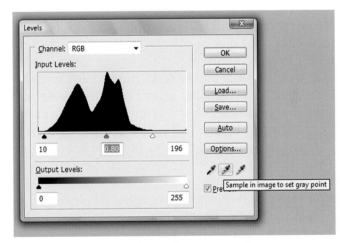

- Open the Levels dialogue box as described earlier.
- The left-hand eyedropper is used to set the black point (darkest part) and the right-hand eyedropper for the white point (brightest part).
- Click on the middle eyedropper to select a part of the image which should be grey.

Using eyedroppers for colour corrections

4. Cropping the image

To crop and rotate an image are basic steps. If your image is not straight it may be that you have either scanned an image that was not quite square on the scanner or that you did not have the camera perfectly horizontal when you took the photograph.

1. Select the 'Crop' tool from the Toolbox.
2. Draw a box around the area that is approximately how you want your composition to look.
3. Adjust the position of the corners and edges as needed. Everything that is outside this crop window will be removed when you complete the crop command.
4. To rotate the crop window, position the mouse cursor just outside a corner of the box so that a 'rotate' icon is displayed for the mouse cursor. You can then freely rotate the box left or right as needed.
5. Press 'Enter' to perform the final crop or click on the tick mark in the Options bar.

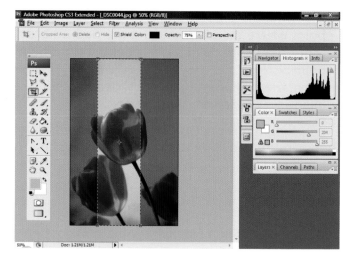

5. Saving images and graphics

This step saves your edited graphics and/or images onto your computer hard disk or other suitable location. It is a good idea to save a full-size, high-resolution image as your master file together with a smaller file (lower resolution image with less pixels) for use with email or for smaller print purposes. By default, the graphics will most likely be saved in the original format for JPG files, but changed to PSD if using layers. This is because JPG files do not support the use of layers. If you select the JPG file type then, at the bottom of the 'Save' box in Adobe PhotoShop, you can find an approximation of the final file size and how long it would take to send by email. An alternative to reducing the number of pixels for a smaller file size is to reduce the JPG quality, but don't forget to save this as a separate file rather than overwriting your high-resolution image. Once pixels or image quality are discarded, they cannot be recovered. From the 'File' menu – click on 'Save As'. Refer to the notes on suitable file formats earlier in this chapter depending on what the graphic will be used for.

Objective (3c)

Objective (3d)

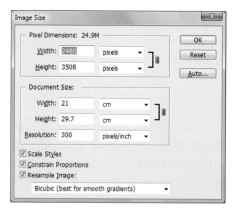

If saving an image for use on the Web, the pixel dimensions needed are unlikely to be any higher than 800 pixels wide and the resolution should be set to 72dpi.

If saving for print use, the pixel dimensions will need to be high enough for the required document print size at a resolution of 300dpi. So, for example, an A4 page for printing at 21cm × 29.7cm is shown in the image size dialogue box (above).

Additional image processing tools and techniques

Sharpening

Most digital images and graphics will benefit from sharpening before making a final print. This should be done at the very last moment before printing and the values chosen will depend on the print size and resolution. It is best not to save a file that has already been sharpened as your master file, as the next time you want to produce a print it may be for a different size and resolution – hence the sharpening values might need to be different.

Printing

When printing the final photographs and graphics, use the print preview to check what they will look like first. This is especially important if you are planning to use photographic-quality paper and large full-colour prints, which can be costly to produce. In Adobe PhotoShop use the 'File' menu, then 'Print preview' to see exactly what will be printed on the final page. You can adjust the size and position of the image prior to using high-quality paper for your printed photographs. You will also need to set the printer properties correctly for the paper and quality required, for example, 'best photo' and 'glossy' paper.

1 Objective (3c)

Editing and retouching tools

After the basic workflow techniques have been applied, there is a wide range of tools and techniques that can be used in Adobe PhotoShop to produce creative images and graphics. The main ones are described in this next section, which are only required at level 2.

Note: There are often multiple tools on the tool icons. Click and hold on one of the tools to see a list of alternatives.

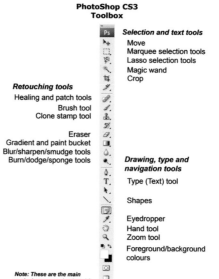

2 Objective (3c)

Cloning Tool

The purpose of the clone stamp is to copy parts of the image from one section into a different section. This is a very useful tool that can be used to remove unwanted details from a photograph although practise is needed to build up your skill level.

To use the clone tool:

- Click on the icon in the tool box once to select it.
- If needed, select the brush style from the 'options' bar although the soft-edged default brush works well on most images.
- Set the required brush size (also in the 'options' bar) by dragging the slider up or down. A useful keyboard shortcut for brush sizes is the left and right square brackets [ ] to decrease and increase size respectively.
- Move the mouse onto the image and position it close to the feature that you want to remove, then press and hold down the 'Alt' key so that the mouse cursor changes to a 'target' icon.

- Single click with the left mouse button, then release the 'Alt' key.
- Carefully move the mouse across the image onto the part to be removed, remembering where you have just clicked for the clone source point.
- Click and hold down the left mouse button so that a cross hair and a circle are shown as mouse cursors. The tool works by copying the colour information from the cross hair (source) and pasting it into the circle (destination). When using this tool, keep an eye on both of these.
- Keep repositioning the source point as needed using 'Alt' click for different parts of the image to be modified and try to avoid repeat patterns.

The above image was originally a portrait photograph and has been duplicated to give a symmetrical mirrored image (although the person has been cloned out of the right-hand side).

Healing and patching

 Later versions of PhotoShop Elements have healing but not the patch tool, although Creative Suite has both. You can use the healing brushes to remove small blemishes and spots by blending the colours and textures.

 The patch tool is a large area healing brush and is used by first drawing a shape with the mouse. This area can be used as the 'source' or 'destination' for the blending.

Retouching tools

Smudge, blur and sharpen

Smudge tool

 This is a good way to 'push' colours around. Think of an oil painting when the oils are still wet – you could push the colours around with a finger. This is what the smudge tool does – just click and hold the left mouse button down and push in the direction you want. This tool can be useful when repairing old photographs, although for most work you are more likely to use the clone stamp.

Blur tool

 The blur tool does exactly what it says – blurs the area under the cursor. You can use this for softening edges but anything larger is best done using one of the blur options in the filter menu (such as Gaussian blur, which has variable control)

Sharpen tool

 This does the opposite of blurring, but again is best limited to use on edges. Don't overdo this otherwise you can produce some pretty horrible edges to the subjects of your picture. For larger areas, you can also use the sharpening options in the filter menu (such as the unsharp mask, which has variable control).

Dodge, burn and sponge tools

Dodge tool:

 The name comes from a darkroom technique whereby the light is restricted from reaching the photographic paper. This makes the image lighter.

Burn tool

 The name of this tool also comes from the darkroom and is the opposite to the dodge tool. It allows more light to reach the paper, and this makes it darker. Both the burn and dodge tools are best used on monochrome (black and white images) in small amounts. Try removing the colour from an image and use the burn tool on the highlights at 10–20 per cent. Likewise, try the dodge tool on the shadows with a similar setting of 10–20 per cent.

Sponge tool

 This is used to change the colour saturation of selected parts of the image. In CS3, change the mode between saturate and desaturate depending on whether you want to increase or decrease the intensity of the colour. If you want to apply this to the whole image, you can use the hue/saturation adjustment sliders from the 'Image' menu – 'Adjustments'.

Red eye tool

If photographs have been taken with flash of people or animals looking into the camera, they can sometimes suffer from 'red eye'. There is a special tool to remove this effect and replace the red with a more natural colour. Using PhotoShop CS3, you can just click and drag the tool over the red eye to automatically fix this. Other versions have a colour replacement brush to click on selected parts that need to be removed.

Selection tools

Selection tools allow you to define parts of the image so that you can make changes to them without affecting the whole image.

Alternatively, selections can be copied and pasted into other images to build up a montage.

An active selection area appears with a flashing dotted line around it, sometimes referred to as 'marching ants'.

The toolbox includes drawing selection tools for use with shapes, and colour selection tools for use with a specific range or luminosity of colours. Brushes can also be used to create or modify selections. PhotoShop Elements uses a paint brush technique to define all areas for selection. Areas can be added or

Dotted lines show the background selected

subtracted by using either the 'selection' or 'mask' option. In PhotoShop CS versions, a similar process uses quick mask mode and the normal brush tool with the foreground/background colours set to black/white.

Marquee

 These use either rectangular or elliptical shapes for regular-shaped outlines in the image. If you hold down the 'Shift' key at the same time, this will enable you to draw a perfect square or circle.

Lasso

There are three different types of lasso tool:

- The freehand lasso tool works like a pencil on the screen – it follows the mouse when you hold the left mouse button down. Releasing the mouse button joins up the start and end points. It is sometimes useful for adding extra bits into a selection that have been missed out.
- The polygonal tool draws straight lines between mouse click points.
- The magnetic lasso tool attempts to trace the outline of an object by automatically recognising the edges. It works best when there is good contrast between the object you want to select and the background. If you make a mistake in the edge, use the delete key to remove the previous anchor point. This is a good selection tool to become familiar with and learn how to use effectively. There

are three settings in the options bar to improve the performance of this tool:

- Edge contrast is the value that a pixel has to differentiate it from its adjacent pixel and be recognised as the edge.
- Width is the number of pixels either side of the pointer used to find the edge.
- Frequency is the distance between the fastening or anchor points.

Magic wand

 This selection tool uses colour or luminosity to recognise which pixels are to be selected. The options bar has a checkbox to control whether these are either contiguous (all joined together) or non-contiguous (anywhere on the image as long as it is within the colour tolerance).

New/add/subtract/intersect (found on the options toolbar)

Having created an initial selection, you can add extra areas or remove them using one of these modes. They are available with all selection tools, so, for example, you could use a magic wand selection to start with, change to the lasso and choose the 'add to selection' to carry on adding extra parts of the image.

PRACTICE EXERCISE

Using selection tools with filters and effects

1. Open a photographic image that has a single main subject (see example opposite).
   a. Use a suitable selection tool(s) on the main subject.
   b. Invert the selection from the 'Select – Inverse' menu option.
   c. Remove the colour from the rest of the image.

Photo with colour removed from background

Drawing and painting tools

Gradient

 This is best created on a new layer to allow editing and further modification. When editing photographs, using the 'foreground colour to transparent' can be one of the most useful. Alternatively, when creating original graphics from a blank worksheet, the two colour gradients provide more dynamic visual effects than plain colours.

Brush

 The brush can be used with quick masks and for freehand painting of shapes.

Pencil

 The pencil draws thin lines, similar to a very narrow brush.

Shapes

These are created as vector-based graphics and so are scalable for any resolution. There is a library of shapes built into all versions of Adobe PhotoShop in several categories.

Eraser tool

 This is used to permanently erase parts of a layer that are not wanted. Consider whether it would be better to use selection tools instead of just erasing a background, although the eraser can also be used to tidy up the edges of selections when using layers.

Text (type) tool

This allows you to add text to images such as titles and/or descriptions. The text and images are placed in separate layers so they can always be modified later. Text is based on vector graphics, meaning that it can be scaled to any size and still maintain a smooth outline. Having first clicked on the Text tool, move the cursor onto the image where you want the text to start and click the mouse again. Type your text using the keyboard. You can change the font and colour from the 'Options' bar.

Changing the foreground/background colours

At the bottom of the Toolbox can be found the foreground and background colour boxes. Click inside each box to display the colour picker window to choose a new colour. The default colours (black/white) can be set by clicking the smaller icon at the side. The colours can be exchanged by clicking the two-way arrow.

Specific tools and techniques found in the menus

Undo

Undo is a common Microsoft Windows® toolbar icon and found in Adobe PhotoShop Elements, although Adobe PhotoShop CS variants have a much more powerful and flexible history palette. This is used to reverse the previous actions or edits if errors have been made. Adobe PhotoShop Elements has a shortcut on the main toolbar for this.

Transformation techniques

One example of a use for this technique is to straighten the perspective of photographs:

First of all you must select the entire image from 'Select' > 'Select all'. From the 'Edit' menu, click on 'Transform' using one of the options provided. In addition to using the 'Transform' menu, you can also use 'Ctrl' click on any of the corners to adjust the individual transformation points.

Before:	After:

Shadow/Highlight

This is provided in Adobe PhotoShop Elements Version 3 onwards and Adobe PhotoShop CS.

If photos have been taken in strong sunlight, the bright areas (highlights) can be very bright and the dark areas (shadows) very dark. This creates an image with very high contrast, in which case the shadow/highlight control can improve this. Click on 'Image' > 'adjustments' > 'shadow/highlight control'. Don't overdo this: 10–20 per cent changes are OK but the default of 50 per cent is quite harsh and can introduce noise effects in the shadows.

Changing image or canvas size

Always keep a high-resolution image as your master file. From this, change the image size or crop it to the required dimensions and resolution needed by the client or project. A low-resolution version is also much easier to send by email for proofing purposes. You can check or modify the image size and resize it from the 'Image' menu > 'Resize' > 'Image size'. A box appears as shown (right):

This shows the number of pixels in the image and the printed document size for a given resolution (i.e. number of pixels per inch). You can change the number of pixels, print size or resolution that is suitable for sending by email. Each of the field boxes are linked and changing one field will have an effect on the others at the same time. Make sure all the settings are as you need before clicking on 'OK'.

Using filters

Knowledge of these editing techniques is required for Level 1. There is a large range of filters available in Adobe PhotoShop, some basic examples would be:

- Distort
- Liquify
- Artistic (Watercolour, Paint daubs)
- Blur
- Distort

PRACTICE EXERCISE (LEVELS 1 AND 2)

Using selection tools with filters and effects

1. Using a photographic image of your own choice (or one from the resource CD), use a range of filters from categories such as:
   a. Liquify
   b. Artistic – Smudge stick and/or Watercolour
   c. Sketch.

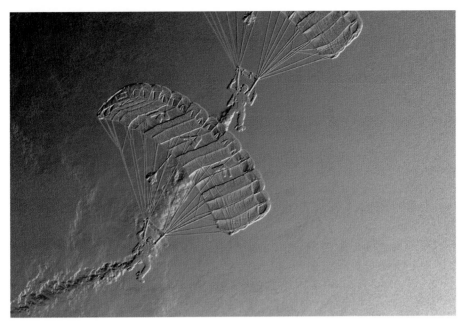

Photo with bas relief filter

Using layers

The layers palette shows how an image is constructed – a new photograph will have just a single background layer. Each layer can be thought of as a sheet of glass or acetate that is transparent in the parts that are shown as a checkerboard pattern. Imagine you are looking down on these layers from the top – the top layer is seen first and you will be able to see through all the transparent areas.

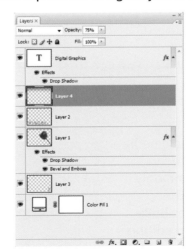

Individual layers can be added, turned off for editing, renamed or moved. Contents can also be changed and skilful use of layers is a great way to create montages.

Using other software

The screen layout varies but the four basic sections are:

1. Workspace/editing window
2. Menus

3. Toolbars with shortcut icons
4. Tools panel

The basic processes and concepts of creating digital graphics are the same whichever software is being used. These are:

1. Transfer the images from camera to computer.
2. Open images, check image quality.
3. Adjust brightness/contrast or Levels.
4. Adjust/correct colours.
5. Save with a descriptive filename in a suitable high-quality format.
6. Additional editing techniques may be used and new files created. Save the final work with the pixel dimensions and resolution required.

When using different software for the first time, identify how to do the basics and then build your knowledge of the extra features as needed. There are a number of other software options for graphics editing. We will take a brief look at some of these on the following pages.

Using Adobe PhotoShop on an Apple Mac computer

When using Adobe PhotoShop on an Apple Mac computer, the keyboard control keys and menus are slightly different.

1. The Microsoft Windows® key is the equivalent of the Apple Command key.
2. PhotoShop menus are slightly different. The functions from the Microsoft Windows® File menu are split between a file menu and 'Apple' menu.

Other software options for editing graphics

Adobe (Macromedia) Fireworks

This was originally a Macromedia graphics editing software application that was commonly used alongside Flash and Dreamweaver. It provides both bitmap and vector-based editing tools, supporting layers and a range of options for exporting web-ready graphics.

At the top of the workspace window you can find the tabs to

preview exported files. These compare the original image quality with the export format and file size.

When a tool is selected from the toolbox, the tool options are displayed in the tool properties at the bottom of the workspace. Using the selection tool, you can also right-click on an image and convert to a symbol or animate movement (see Chapter 4 Digital animation for more information on these processes). If creating graphics for the Web, animation or gaming purposes, use the 'optimize and align' panel at the right-hand side. This allows you to use optimization techniques for the file size, quality and export format. The 'layers' panel works in the same way as PhotoShop layers.

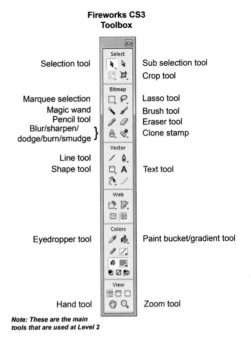

Fireworks CS3 Toolbox

Selection tool	Sub selection tool
	Crop tool
Marquee selection	Lasso tool
Magic wand	Brush tool
Pencil tool	Eraser tool
Blur/sharpen/dodge/burn/smudge }	Clone stamp
Line tool	
Shape tool	Text tool
Eyedropper tool	Paint bucket/gradient tool
Hand tool	Zoom tool

Note: These are the main tools that are used at Level 2

Apple iPhoto

The adjustment tools in Apple iPhoto offer a similar range of basic editing techniques as PhotoShop. These include:

- brightness/contrast
- colour and saturation
- sharpness
- Levels histogram
- filter effects.

Move the sliders to make any necessary adjustments, checking the Levels histogram as you work. Try to keep the red, blue and green curves inside the window, otherwise you will be clipping some colour and tone information.

Workspace from Apple iPhoto, which combines image library management and basic editing tools and effects, which are ideal for Level 1.

PART 4: REVIEWING YOUR WORK

When reviewing digital graphics work there will be a number of questions to ask:

1. Does the content of the final image/graphic show what the client actually wanted?
2. Is the graphic file size suitable for the client and target audience?
3. Is the graphic file format suitable for the client and target audience (e.g. web or print)?
4. Is the image quality suitable in terms of exposure, sharpness of focus, colour and composition?
5. Is the *editing* of the graphics effective and pleasing to look at?
6. Does the final work demonstrate a conventional or creative/innovative approach? There is no right or wrong here – just recognise what has been produced.
7. What improvements could be made – for example camera equipment, composition and/or editing techniques?

> 1 Objective (4a)

> 2 Objective (4a)

You may want to obtain some constructive comments from friends and the client in order to answer these questions. You could also refer to the general comments in the section on Planning and Review in the Introduction.

SUMMARY

Developing skills with the basic workflow and editing tools will enable you to create a wide range of digital graphics from your images. Maybe you will have experimented with several other tools and techniques along the way in addition to this basic set. Perhaps this will even inspire you to progress onto higher levels of study to develop your creative talents further. Let's hope so!

FINAL ASSIGNMENT

Once you have learned all the required parts of the unit, you will complete an assignment that will be used to assess your knowledge and skills of the subject. It will be set in a vocational context, which means that it will simulate what it would be like to be given a project by a client or employer in a work situation. To start you should read the brief or scenario carefully to identify what is needed. A typical assignment may be in the following format (although these should not be used as templates for designing your own assignments – refer to the guidance documents on the OCR website for this purpose):

Brief:
You are a junior designer for Tulipa Rossa sports goods and have been asked to produce an image for use on the new website. For this you will need to obtain a series of photographs that show sports equipment and combine these with text for the Tulipa brand name. The client has requested that the image is 600 pixels wide by 400 pixels high and be in a suitable file format/resolution for web use.

Task 1: Here you may be asked to explore the type of camera and features needed to capture the photographs. You will also consider what suitable file formats and settings will be used for both capturing the photographs and creating the final work.

Task 2: In this task you will be asked to plan the development of your work. Use one or more of the planning methods described in the Introduction, identifying what you will need and how long it is likely to take. The composition and layout of the work should be considered and a visualization diagram or sketch produced of what the final image should look like.

Task 3: In this task you will be asked to actually produce or create your work. This should demonstrate a range of skills using the camera and image editing software.

Task 4: In this task you should review your final work. This means thinking about things like overall quality, fitness for purpose and any areas for improvement. It is not just a summary of how you created the work – it should be a reflection by yourself (and others) on how suitable it is for use by the client described in the brief.

Note that essential parts of the assignment include the planning and reviewing of your work. It is important to be able to think about what you need to produce and what the final work should look like. Since the assignment is in a vocational context it will be important to check the suitability of what you have produced before submitting it to the client. The development of these skills will be a great benefit when you are asked to produce something in the real/commercial world of employment.

Web Authoring

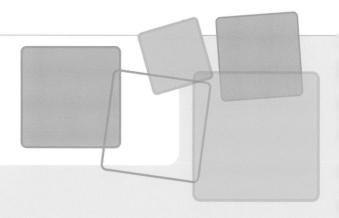

The aim of this unit is to learn how to design and create websites. It begins with how to access the World Wide Web, website structure and the use of site maps. You will develop skills in combining text and graphics with working site navigation to produce a functional website.

1 Unit 2

2 Unit 2

PART 1: WEBSITE STRUCTURE AND HOW TO ACCESS THE INTERNET

Traditionally, websites were accessed using a computer connected to the Internet via a modem and a standard telephone line. Today we have much faster broadband connections, which make it possible to include sound, streaming video, animation and other rich media features. The way we access the Internet is also undergoing change. Many mobile phones now have larger colour screens with higher resolution that can connect to the World Wide Web. Both mobile phone and PDA (Personal Digital Assistant) devices can display enough information to be useful as portable web browsers. Websites are now being designed to detect what hardware is being used to view them. Hence the website can supply the content in a page layout and format suitable for the mobile phone or computer that is being used to access it.

2 Objective (1a)

Websites can be created using HTML editors such as Adobe Dreamweaver, Microsoft FrontPage®, Expression® and SharePoint®. There are a growing number of Flash websites, which may not use HTML at all. These are created using Adobe Flash (formerly

Macromedia Flash) and enable advanced rich media sites to be produced that combine sound, video and animation.

Technology devices used to access the Internet

Platform	Features
Computer	Requires web browser software with broadband, cable or wireless access. There are some security risks which can be minimised using anti-virus and firewall software. Display devices such as a monitor or LCD are a good size.
Mobile phone	Display screens are now larger and in colour. Connection speeds and the cost per MB of data downloaded can be restrictive.
PDA	Personal digital assistant, usually with a larger screen than a mobile phone.

Connecting to the Internet

Broadband

Broadband is a term used to describe any high-speed connection such as DSL/ADSL and cable. Speeds are typically between 2Mbps and 8Mbps or more for DSL, depending on location. Cable connections provide speeds of up to 30Mbps.

Dial-up modem

This is a hardware device used in between a computer and a standard telephone line. A special number is dialled to connect to an ISP (Internet service provider), which allows data communications instead of voice to be used. Speeds are relatively slow, up to 56kbps.

Cable modems

These are supplied with cable television connections, typically up to 30Mbps, providing a very fast connection speed.

Wireless

Many laptop computers are now fitted with wireless connectivity. These can connect to a broadband modem/router in the home or workplace. Wireless hot spots and open zones can also be found at airports, hotels and on trains.

Mobile networks

Access to the Internet is available from mobile phones with GPRS connectivity and a WAP browser.

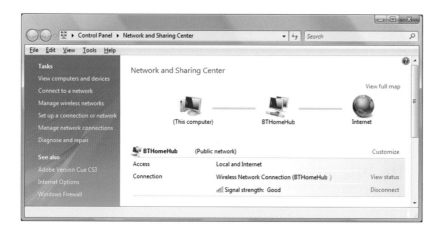

Note: Connection speed is measured in kilobits per second (kbps) or megabits per second (Mbps). Download speeds are usually faster than upload speeds. For example a 4Mb download speed may have typically 0.5Mb upload speed. Expected times needed to transfer files to or from the Internet are shown in the following table, which you will need to be aware of when thinking about uploading your work to the e-Portfolio:

File size (megabytes)	Connection speed (upload or download)		
	256Kb (kilobits)	1Mb (megabit)	4Mb (megabit)
1MB	32 seconds	8 seconds	2 seconds
4MB	2.1 minutes	32 seconds	8 seconds
20MB	10.7 minutes	2.7 minutes	40 seconds
50MB	26.7 minutes	6.7 minutes	1.7 minutes

In practice, the times quoted may be slightly longer due to the additional information that must also be sent, for example how the data is to be used and where it should be sent to. When checking the file size, your computer will show the size in kilobytes (KB) or megabytes (MB) rather than kilobits or megabits. There are 8 bits in one byte, so a 1MB (megabyte) file has 8 Mb (megabits). Note that a bit is shown as a small 'b' whereas a byte is shown as a capital 'B'.

Purpose and benefits of a website

Websites are provided for businesses, organisations and individuals. The main uses are:

- providing information
- education
- entertainment
- selling goods and/or services.

The benefits to providers of well-designed websites are that they are low maintenance, low cost (once created) and available to users 24 hours a day, seven days a week.

PRACTICE EXERCISE

Explore and review websites

1. Collect some website names (also known as domains or URLs).
2. View each of the websites using a computer, web browser and Internet connection.
3. Identify the main purpose of the websites, e.g. information, education, advertising, sales.
4. List approximately how many different sections there are to the site, even if it is difficult to find out how many pages there are in total.
5. Compare how the site navigation works for each site.
6. Compare the different fonts, styles and colours of the page layout.
7. Summarise your findings and list the websites that:
   i) work best (ease of navigation)
   ii) look good (fonts, colours, styles and layout).

HTML is hypertext markup language and represents the code used to create web pages. HTML files contain text with a series of markup tags that inform a web browser how to display the information. You will learn about some basic HTML tags later in this chapter but, for now, try the next exercise as an introduction.

View HTML code and tags in a web browser

1. Choose one of your favourite websites.
2. View the website on the Internet.
3. From the 'View' menu of the web browser – click on 'View source'.
4. Scroll down the page to identify the *header* information and the main *body* of the page code and tags.
5. Be impressed (even if only a little bit).

PART 2: PLAN A WEBSITE STRUCTURE

Planning a website to a client brief

Read or discuss the client brief or specification carefully. Think about how to satisfy the needs of the client using your own creative talents and ideas. Note down ideas on how to meet the needs of the client using good web design principles. Part of your planning will overlap with the development of the site map and page layout. Discuss all ideas with the client before starting to code the pages. Visualization diagrams and sketches are one of the best ways to plan your work for this subject. Refer to the section on Planning and Review in the Introduction, which includes sections on how to conceptualize, visualize and storyboard your work.

2 Objective (2a)

Page content and layout

When planning the web page layout, you can use visualization sketches to illustrate your ideas. An example would be:

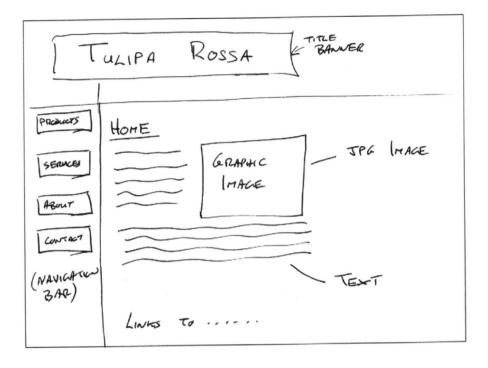

This sketch shows a main banner at the top of the page, navigation at the left-hand side with the main body in the middle. This is a fairly common and conventional layout for web pages. By producing a layout sketch for each page in the website, you will be able to identify where to use list formats and tables, together with any internal and external hyperlinks. This planning phase is also used to identify what colour schemes, fonts and text styles will be used in the website. These aspects of the website are best defined in a master page – or one that will be used to standardise the style of all pages in the website. Depending on what software you are using and whether it is for Level 1 or Level 2, your master page could be a simple page layout, template, theme or cascading style sheet (CSS). More on these options is discussed later in this chapter.

By considering the layout of each page, you will able to list what assets will be needed to build the site, for example text information, images, graphics and animation files. These will need to be resized to the required pixel dimensions and resolution before being placed on the web pages. Information on how to prepare graphics for web use can be found in Chapter 2 Digital Graphics.

Of course you will need to document any use of copyrighted, trademarked or intellectual property. Keep records of all sources and permissions obtained for any material that is not your own. You may also need model and/or property releases from any people and property that may be identified in your work. Examples of these releases can be found on the resource CD and are used to show that you have permission to use any images or graphics on your web site.

Finally, think about how long the whole project will take. After your initial discussions with the client, they will want to know how long it will take to produce the work. Break this down into timescales for site design, development and testing.

Creativity with web authoring

The main aspects to explore here are the page layout and colour schemes. Pale backgrounds with dark text or dark backgrounds with light text will probably work best. Although bright, bold background colours and text may look good at first glance, they may not be ideal for a commercial client or business. You will need to consider the realistic needs of both the client and the target audience when developing your ideas and choosing solutions. This will be an important part of the assignment that you complete at the end of the course, which will be based on a client brief that asks you to develop a website for a given purpose.

Creating a site map

After you have found out what your client needs from a website, one of the first steps is to draw a site map.

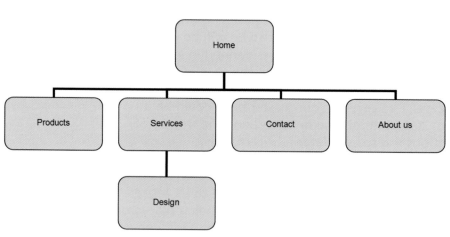

An example of a site map

The site map shows how many pages will be produced for the website and how they link together. The navigation will identify the route through the website to get to a particular page. In the example above, to display the 'Design' page you will need to navigate from 'Home' through 'Services'.

- *Parent page*: defined as the page above the current page.
- *Child page*: defined as the page below the current page.

For example, 'Design' is a child page of 'Services' and the parent page for 'Services' is the 'Home' page.

PART 3: CREATING A WEBSITE

Having designed the basic website structure and identified the page content, the next step is to develop these into a website using web authoring software tools.

 Objective (3a)

 Objective (3a)

Development software options

Software application	Comments
Adobe (Macromedia) Dreamweaver	Professional-level development software
Microsoft FrontPage® Microsoft Expression Web®	Professional-level development software
Adobe GoLive®	Early Adobe Creative Suite application before their merger with Macromedia
NVU	An open source web development software application provided under the Mozilla public licence
Serif Webplus®	High-level web design application with support for e-commerce sites
Apple iWeb®	Apple Mac web development software application, part of the iLife suite

It is possible to create websites using word-processing applications and even Microsoft Windows® Notepad. However, this qualification is looking to develop skills in industry-standard web authoring software. When building your website, you will need to include the main components of web pages, which are:

- text
- graphics
- hyperlinks
- navigation.

Folder structure and naming conventions

Development folders for storing files and assets should be under one web folder. Pages with HTML code are normally stored in the root folder with images and style sheets in separate folders underneath this. The filenames for each page should describe the content such as:

- *index.htm or default.htm*: the first page of the website (sometimes 'home.htm' but 'index.htm' is a more universal reference name)
- *about.htm*: describes information about the company or owner of the website
- *products.htm*: describes what products are offered by the company or owner
- *services.htm*: describes what services are offered by the company or owner
- *contact.htm*: identifies how to contact the company or owner, with address, telephone, email and possibly a location map

Additional pages in the website should also have appropriate names. The folder structure will depend on the software being used, but it is likely to store images in a dedicated '*_images*' folder for instance. You should aim to put all of your images and graphics in this folder at the start of the site development.

   Note: Do not use spaces, apostrophes or other special characters in file names. These can cause problems with the hosting server depending on what operating system it uses. Keep to letters, numbers and hyphens/underscores.

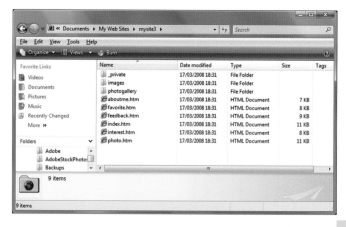

In this next section, you will learn the basic principles of building a website using a high-level web authoring software application.

Using Adobe Dreamweaver

The following section describes the basic steps and tools of using Adobe Dreamweaver. Dreamweaver was developed originally by Macromedia and taken over by Adobe in 2005. The screen captures in this section are taken from Dreamweaver CS3 although previous versions have similar menus and layout. The Dreamweaver workspace is shown below:

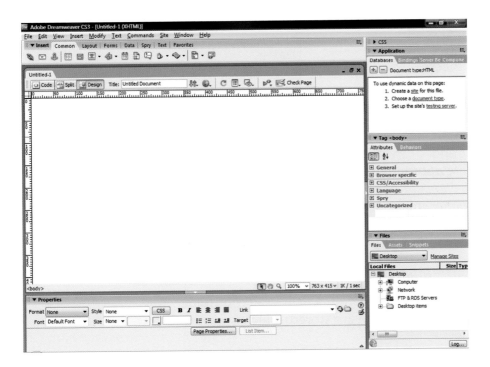

At the bottom of the workspace is the 'Properties' panel.

This panel shows the relevant information for the current selected item in the web page. To make changes to any item, click on the item to select it and then modify the properties as needed.

Panels

Panels are found at the right-hand side of the workspace. There are four standard panels displayed at start-up, although these can be customised for the workspace and development tasks:

- CSS: The CSS panel is for developing websites with cascading style sheets.
- Application
- Tag: The TAG panel enables you to set the attributes for a range of parameters such as browser specific and accessibility (more appropriate to Level 3).
- Files: The Files panel will be used to manage the files and folders in your website.

To create a new Dreamweaver site

You can produce a new site by creating a new local root folder. This is where all of the files for the site are stored, which is managed from the Files panel.

From the 'Site' menu, select 'New'. The site definition process must be completed in order to be able to use templates (see later section). Note that you do not have to decide on the HTTP address (or URL) of the finished website at this stage. The purpose of storing all of the files and assets in one root folder is to make sure that all navigation links and images work correctly when published by using relative links and references (more on this later). The basic process is to build the site locally and then publish to its hosted location.

The Dreamweaver interface includes an 'Insert' bar below the main menus. This bar provides access to frequently used features in the 'Common' section.

This 'Insert' bar is used when inserting components onto web pages.

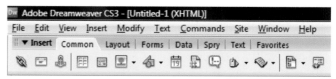

Creating and using a master page

For the purposes of Level 1 and Level 2, a master page is defined as a standard page layout that is used on all pages in the website. This master page defines the page background colour, the font styles and colours, navigation bars and title banners. Any areas that are common to all pages are defined in this master page. Depending on what software is actually being used, the type of master page may be a template, theme or possibly cascading style sheet (CSS) which is described later in this chapter. At Level 1 the master page can be created as a standard single page, which is then opened each time a new web page is created (then re-saved with a new name such as index.htm, about.htm, and so on).

2 Objective (3a)

The purpose of using a master page is to make sure that the whole website has a similar 'look' and 'feel' to it. This uniformity is something you may have noticed when exploring a range of websites earlier on. Professional-looking sites have easy-to-read pages, with clear colour schemes and fonts.

All pages that have a similar content will use the same style and layout. If you are developing a website for Level 2 using a master page, the aim is that the style of the whole website can be changed by modifying a single style page instead of having to open and edit every page individually.

To explore the capabilities and features of page creation in Dreamweaver, create a simple html page as follows. From the 'File' menu select 'New'. Alternatively, click on HTML from the start-up screen.

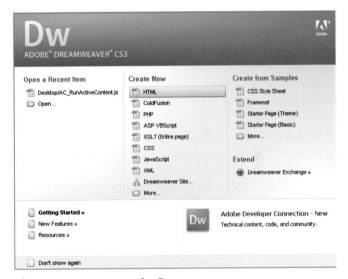

The start-up screen in Dreamweaver

Editing the page properties and style

With a blank page displayed in the workspace, select the 'Modify' menu and click on 'Page properties'.

The appearance category covers the text fonts, background colours and margins. Choose the new settings that you would like and click on the 'Apply' button to preview what the page will look like. If you are using this as the master page, select 'File' > 'Save As' and type in a name such as *master.htm*.

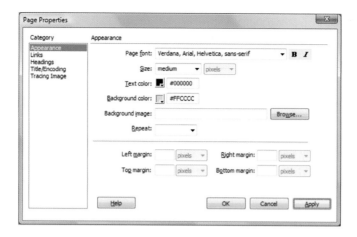

Creating a website using a Dreamweaver template (Level 2 only)

Templates in Dreamweaver offer a range of standard page designs, some of which have editable regions. This is useful if you are working with a group of people and only want them to have access to certain sections of the page. For example, you may want to define the top banner section of the page and the navigation bar as uneditable regions. The main body for page text and graphics would need to be defined as editable and then the page saved as a template. Once a template page has been opened, to create an editable region, right-click with the mouse and select 'templates' > 'editable region'. Note that all regions in a template are initially defined as uneditable.

Another feature of Dreamweaver templates is that they can be used to update every page in a website that uses the template; that is, modifications to the template are globally and automatically applied to each page that is based on the template.

To produce a template, create a HTML page in the layout and style that you want. From the 'File' menu, select 'Save As' and change the 'save as type' field to be a template .dwt file. Alternatively, if you are creating the template page from scratch, you can choose 'File' > 'New' > 'HTML template'. In order to use templates in a Dreamweaver site, you must have completed the site definition and have created a root folder in which to store the file.

A CSS (cascading style sheet) is another way to standardise the layout of all pages in a website. Building a website based on CSS means that the appearance of all pages on the site is defined by an external style sheet. All you need to do is modify this one single style sheet and the whole site will be updated automatically to the new text, font and colour schemes. If your website does not use CSS or a template, it would be necessary to open every page of the website separately to change the background colour or any other attribute and re-save them one at a time. Dreamweaver has a range of built-in CSS layouts. These can be seen from 'File' menu > 'New' > 'HTML' and the available CSS layouts will be displayed.

Creating a navigation bar

A navigation bar provides an easy way for the user of a website to navigate between the site pages by clicking on a button or text field.

1 Objective (2b)

A navigation bar can be created in the master page, template or any individual site page.

From the common category of the insert bar, click on the 'images' icon > 'Navigation Bar'. Alternatively, select the 'Insert' menu > 'Image objects' >'Navigation Bar'.

You may need to prepare the graphics for the navigation buttons, which can be completed as part of the digital graphics unit. These should be saved in the site root folder in a separate folder such as '_images'.

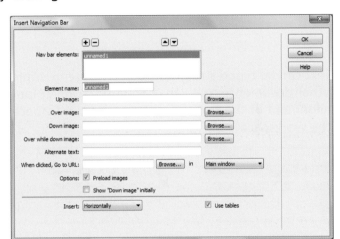

Manage the website structure using site management tools

All the site pages, images and other files are stored using a folder structure under the root. This is to make sure that Dreamweaver can manage and update the links between images and pages when they are changed or modified. To keep the links intact, always use the Files panel to either move or rename the files. File names should still follow the naming conventions mentioned earlier, with no spaces or special characters. The names for each page should also be appropriate to the content.

Using the Files panel

The Files panel can be used after the site definition process is completed. It displays all websites that have been created and managed from within Dreamweaver. You can select any of them from the list without having to go via the normal 'File' > 'Open', 'File > 'Close' menu system.

In the Files panel, you can also drag and drop files into new or different folders. This works in a similar way to Windows Explorer® but, more importantly, the navigation links between website pages will be maintained. After each move, the links to be automatically updated will be summarised for you to accept or reject.

Adding content to a website

Text

Text can be typed straight into each page or copied and pasted from other documents. You can change the font, colour, size and alignment of the text using the properties inspector at the bottom of the workspace.

Use the mouse to select the block of text you want to change. In Properties, choose the required format, font, style, size (small, med, large) and alignment. Headline styles such as <h1> use a larger font to give more structure to the layout of the text.

Images and graphics

Before inserting images and graphics into site pages, place them in a suitable sub-folder of the local root folder in the site such as '_images'. This means that Dreamweaver will be able to manage the paths and links to the image once it is published to a remote destination server. If you just insert the image from an external folder such as *My pictures*, an absolute link will be created, which means that the image may not be displayed on the published site, because it will be stored on a different computer.

To insert an image, select the insert common bar and click on the image icon. Browse to the folder containing your image, click to select it and then on the 'OK' button.

After the image has been placed on the web page, left-click the mouse once on the image and view the properties in the inspector at the bottom of the screen. This allows you to set the image attributes, alignment, alt text and cropping. Optimization is only available in CS3.

The size of a photograph may need to be optimized before finishing the website. If you are using an original image from a digital camera, it may be several megapixels in size. Web graphics do not need this resolution because a typical display screen may only be 800 or 1024 pixels wide. You can change the size of an image on the page just by clicking and dragging a corner – leaving the file size the same, which does not optimize the graphic for page load times. It is generally better to prepare all images and graphics in a digital graphics editing application first, before placing them on website pages.

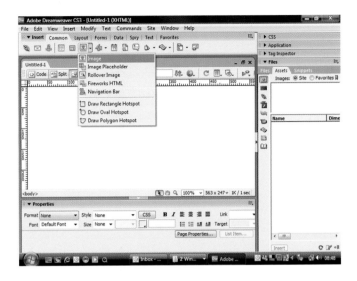

Lists and tables

A numbered or bulleted list is an easy way to present information on a web page in a clear format. To create an unordered bullet list, choose the 'ul' from the common text bar. Otherwise you can just type in the text first and use the properties inspector to change the style to be a numbered or unordered bulleted list.

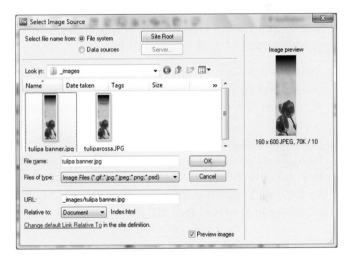

Tables can be inserted onto a page from the 'Insert' menu > 'Table'. Alternatively, there is a table icon on the common insert bar. Create the table with the required number of rows, columns and header that you need. Don't worry if you are not sure to start with – these can be changed later on from the property inspector.

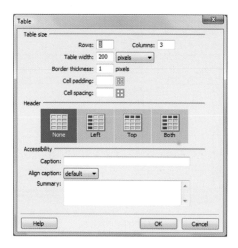

Internal and external hyperlinks

When working with hyperlinks, you will need to know the difference between absolute and relative links:

- **Relative links** are referenced to their location within the root folder and so they should always work in the destination website. A relative link must be used for all internal links for a published website.
- **Absolute links** are used with an external hyperlink and include the full URL. It does not matter where they are called from but the link address must be accessible by the computer platform, such as by having a working Internet connection. An example of an absolute link would be http://www.imedia.ocr.org.uk.

Creating an internal link (that is not part of the navigation bar)

Select the text or image that will have the hyperlink. Either right-click with the mouse and select 'hyperlink' or use the insert common bar > hyperlink icon. Alternatively, you can also use the 'link' field in the property inspector.

Use the browse feature to locate the page or image that the link should point to, click on 'OK' to complete the link.

Note that any text can have a hyperlink attached, for example text like 'click _here_ to go to the contact page'. The word '_here_' can have a hyperlink to a different page containing contact information and will be underlined to identify that it has a hyperlink.

Creating an external hyperlink

As for creating an internal link, select the text or image to start with. In the properties inspector link field, enter the full URL of the external website.

Creating an email link

As for the external link, select the text or image to start with. In the properties inspector link field, click on insert common bar > email link icon and enter the email address. Alternatively (and for images or graphics) in the properties inspector link field, enter the full email address beginning with a 'mailto:' statement, for example, mailto:imedia@tuliparossa.com.

The building blocks of websites: HTML

Examine and edit HTML code using code view

This code can be viewed in Dreamweaver or most other web page development software applications. It can also be viewed on most websites using the web browser 'View source' feature, covered in the second practical exercise of this chapter.

Dreamweaver provides two main views – Design and Code. There is also an option to split the workspace window to display both of these views. Most web development is completed in Design view. You can examine, write and edit the HTML tags by switching to the

Code view using the button at the top left-hand side of the page tab.

Most tags have a start and end tag. For example, to make a section of text **bold** use <b>bold</b>

The <b> begins the use of bold text and the </b> ends the use.

List of basic html tags

Tag	Use and meaning
<html>	In the header information, it informs the browser that the page uses html tags.
<head>	Header reference information that is not displayed in the browser display.
<title>	The content of this is displayed in the browser title bar (at the very top of the browser window).
<body>	The content of this is displayed in the browser page display.
<a href>	hyperlink reference, e.g. <a href='http://www.imedia.ocr.org.uk'>
<b>	starts **bold** text, e.g. <b>iMedia</b> displays **iMedia**.
<i>	starts *italic* text, e.g. <i>iMedia</i> displays *iMedia*.
<p>	For the start of a new paragraph.
<h1>	A text headline format, with <h2>, <h3>, <h4> also used for additional styles.
<img src>	Used to define the source location for an image or graphic, e.g. <img src='graphic.jpg'>
<table>	To define the start of a table, divided in rows <tr> and data cells <td>
<!-- comments >	For comments and explanations in the html code. This is good practice used by the author to document what is happening next so that others can understand the code.

Note: tags can be combined, so that <b><i>iMedia</b></i> would display ***iMedia***.

Early versions of HTML standards also had <u> for underline but it is no longer supported because of the potential confusion with hyperlinks.

PRACTICE EXERCISE

Using a text editor to create a web page

You can type the html tags in a text editor such as notepad to create a new page. Try entering the following, save it as 'mypage.htm' and open it using a web browser (also supplied on the CD).

```
<html>
<head>
<title>My first iMedia web page</title>
</head>
<body>
This page was created using a text editor.
<p>
<b>Produced by:</b> <i>yourname</i>
</body>
</html>
```

Saving web pages

Once your website is finished, you can save it to the local development folder. Check that you have used appropriate naming conventions as described earlier. If not, modify them using the 'Files' panel before saving.

Testing the website functionality

Functionality testing is completed to make sure the website works as expected. The two main things you need to check are the navigation and page display. One approach to functionality testing is to use the site reporting features within Dreamweaver. The results

1 Objective (3a)

2 Objective (3c)

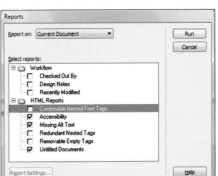

Dreamweaver Reports

1 Objective (4a)

2 Objective (3d)

generated by this process will display a list of problems, errors and warnings as shown (above).

Navigation testing

The main purpose of navigation testing is to make sure that all pages are accessible and there are no broken links. A good approach is to preview the entire site in a browser and check every navigation link, whether in the navigation bar or text/image hyperlinks.
Dreamweaver also has a built-in utility to check for broken links, which is especially useful on larger websites. From the 'Site' menu, select 'Check links sitewide'. The report shows broken links, external links and orphaned files (which have no parent page).

Creating a test plan

A website will have a number of navigation, functions and page display issues that need to be tested before uploading to a web server. The best way to do this is with a test plan document, which lists the tests to be run and the results found.

Test plan			
Test	Criteria for pass/fail	Pass/fail result	Comments
Home page navigation & links	Site navigation and all links work	✓	Internal and external OK
Home page graphics display	Images and graphics correct size and position	✓	
Home page layout	Page layout correct in web browser as designed	✓	Using IE7 and Firefox
Products page navigation & links	Page navigation and all links work	✓	
(continued. . .)			

Preview in a web browser

Not all web browsers handle HTML and CSS in the same way. This is why the pages may look different depending on the type of computer platform, browser and the version used. It therefore becomes important to preview all pages of your website in as many

1 Objective (4a)

browsers as possible. This is a separate task to just previewing the pages from within Dreamweaver. The most popular web browsers are:

- **Internet Explorer®:** Microsoft web browser supplied with the Windows® Operating System
- **Firefox:** Open source web browser developed by Mozilla
- **Opera:** Open source web browser for both Apple Mac and PC
- **Safari®:** Traditionally this was the Apple Mac web browser but it is now also available for PC

To check the page layout and display in a browser window

Either select 'File' menu > 'Preview in Browser' or click on the world globe icon at the top of the page window. Dreamweaver also has a *browser compatibility check* feature. To use this, select the 'File' menu > 'Check page' > 'Browser compatibility'.

Publishing a website

When your website has been completed and fully tested it can be published to a chosen location using Dreamweaver's site publishing tools. These are found in the 'Site' menu > 'Manage sites'.

You can also view the remote site from the Files panel as shown below:

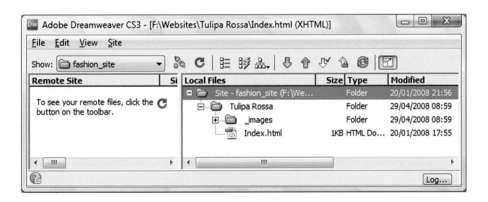

For the purposes of Level 1 and Level 2, you will still need to publish your site to a local network or folder. The contents of the local folder can then be compressed into a single zip file, which is uploaded to the e-Portfolio.

An example of the finished Tulipa Rossa Hair Design website can be found at www.tuliparossa.com.

Other software options for creating websites

Microsoft FrontPage®

Creating a new site using Microsoft FrontPage®

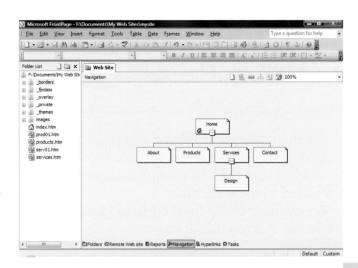

From the 'File' menu, choose 'Blank page', 'From existing page' or 'New website'. There is a range of templates supplied with the authoring software that can be used for your web projects.

You can use a wizard to define the type of new website and the number of pages. Once the wizard has finished, save the website before editing the page content.

Note: The screen shown above is for a new blank page. It can be used to write, examine and edit samples of HTML tags. If the task pane is not shown at the right-hand side, enable it from the 'View' menu.

Microsoft FrontPage® has a graphical site navigation view that displays all of the pages in a website. This is in the same style as the site map developed during the planning phase.

The main functions from this view are:

- Double-click on any page to open it for editing.
- Right-click to rename.
- Click and hold to drag and drop to a different location in the site.

The Folder list at the left-hand side shows the file and folder structure for the local (development) site. Click on any of the pages listed to edit the content.

Site management can also be run from this screen. Click on the 'Remote Web Site' link at the bottom of the display screen window. This will display a split window for both the local and remote site where you can synchronise the content.

In the following screen, a theme has been applied to standardise the style, fonts and colour schemes of all pages in the site (using the 'Format' menu > 'Themes'). At Level 1 and Level 2, themes can be used to standardise the style of all pages in the site. They work using CSS and can be customised to your own requirements. One benefit of using these is that navigation bars and buttons are pre-defined, so they are automatically created from the site map view on the previous page.

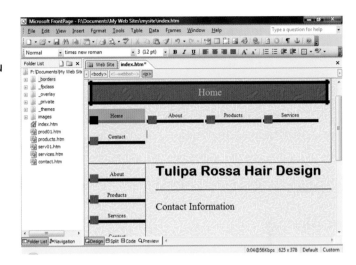

The current screen shown is the standard 'Design' view. At the bottom of the window you can click on the buttons to show the code view or a preview of what the page should look like. This is not quite the same as 'Preview in browser' but usually fairly close. It enables the links to work using the mouse to navigate the site. A 'Preview in browser' function is found on the 'File' menu.

Text can be typed or pasted in as normal using any Microsoft Office® application. Images are inserted using the 'Picture' icon on the standard toolbar or from the 'Insert' menu > 'Picture'.

Nvu

This is an open source web authoring software application for Linux, Windows and Apple Mac computer platforms. Nvu is relatively easy to use and can be freely downloaded. It is distributed under the Mozilla Public Licence (GPL).

Nvu provides a simple toolbar for common functions such as inserting tables, images and hyperlinks. Font styles and properties are shown below the main toolbar. Page layout is set

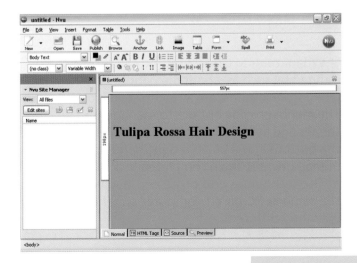

using 'Format' > 'Page colours and background' or 'Page title and properties'. Themes and templates can also be downloaded and used within the authoring software. At the bottom of the workspace you can find the code view (Source) and Preview tabs.

The website is managed using the Nvu Site Manager panel at the left-hand side of the screen.

Apple iWeb

Apple iWeb is part of the iLife suite of software and only available for Apple Mac computers.

When creating a new site, you can choose the purpose from a pre-defined set such as 'about me', photos, movie, blog or podcast. If creating a website from scratch, a blank page layout can also be loaded. The menus provide options to manage the site, insert text, buttons, shapes and hyperlinks. Site and page properties can be modified from the buttons at the bottom right-hand side of the workspace. Site management is again completed in a panel at the left-hand side.

The techniques and processes involved in building a website are the same as PC-based computer systems, although the user interface is slightly different.

PART 4: REVIEW THE WEBSITE

1 Objective (4b)

2 Objective (4a)

The review of your website is the final stage after the functional testing. This should cover basic design principles and the needs of the client and target audience. Consider the following questions:

1. Does the content of the website show what the client actually wanted?
2. Are the text and graphics a suitable size for the client and target audience?
3. Is the download speed appropriate for the expected Internet connection speeds?
4. Is the colour scheme visually pleasing and easy to read? For example, is there good contrast between the text and background colour?
5. Does the final work demonstrate a conventional or creative/innovative approach? There is no right or wrong here – just recognise what has been produced.
6. What improvements could be made? For example, in colours, layout or navigation.

You may want to obtain some constructive comments from friends and the client in order to answer these questions. You could also refer to the general comments in the section on Planning and Review in the Introduction, which includes references to the quality of the finished product, fitness for purpose, constraints and copyright issues.

SUMMARY

By completing this unit, you will have developed skills in producing a website in response to a client brief. You will have identified suitable ways to connect to the website over the Internet and used a site map to record the design process. Having combined text, graphics and navigation on a website, you will have been able to test the functionality and review the layout and colour schemes to make sure that the site meets the needs of the client and target audience.

FINAL ASSIGNMENT

Once you have learned all the required parts of the unit, you will complete an assignment that will be used to assess your knowledge and skills of the subject. It will be set in a vocational context, which means that it will simulate what it would be like to be given a project by a client or employer in a work situation. To start you should read the brief or scenario carefully to identify what is needed. A typical assignment may be in the following format (although these should not be used as templates for designing your own assignments – refer to the guidance documents on the OCR website for this purpose):

> *Brief:*
> *You are a junior web designer for Tulipa Rossa sports goods and have been asked to develop a new website. For this you will need to produce a 4–6 page website using a master page or template that combines text and graphics. Site navigation bars and a banner should be displayed on all the pages.*
> *Task 1: Here you may be asked to explore the features, benefits and purpose of websites.*
> *Task 2: In this task you will be asked to plan the development of your work. Use one or more of the planning methods described in the Introduction, identifying what you will need and how long it is likely to take. A site map must be produced and the layout of sample pages should be shown using a visualization diagram or sketch.*
> *Task 3: In this task you will be asked to actually produce or create your work. This should demonstrate a range of skills using the web authoring software. You will also need to test the finished website to make sure the navigation and text/graphics work correctly.*
> *Task 4: In this task you should review your final work. This means thinking about things like overall quality, fitness for purpose and any areas for improvement. It is not just a summary of how you created the work – it should be a reflection by yourself (and others) on how suitable it is for use by the client described in the brief.*

Note that essential parts of the assignment include the planning and reviewing of your work. It is important to be able to think about what you need to produce and what the final work should look like. Since the assignment is in a vocational context it will be important to check the suitability of what you have produced before submitting it to the client. The development of these skills will be a great benefit when you are asked to produce something in the real/commercial world of employment.

Digital Animation

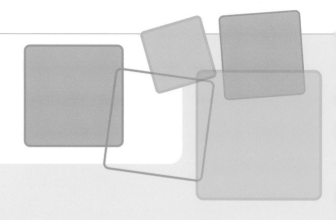

The aim of this unit is to develop knowledge and skills with traditional and digital animation techniques. You will learn how to import images and create your own graphics, which will be called assets in your digital animation software application.

1 Unit 3

2 Unit 2

Animation is defined as a series of static images that give the impression of movement when viewed in quick succession. As a result of completing this unit, you will place graphics onto a digital 'stage' and animate them over a period of time to produce moving images. If you haven't yet created any assets to import into an animation project, you will find some on the CD supplied with this book.

A (very) brief history of animation

Animation has been used largely for entertainment in the form of flip books, cartoons and more recently feature-length films. A plasticine character called Morph appeared with Tony Hart in 1978 and started a new wave of interest in animation that was digitized to produce broadcast-quality short films. Nick Park produced what is now a classic clay modelling animation with the characters Wallace and Gromit. Aardman, Pixar, Dreamworks and Disney have all been pioneers in the development of animated films such as *Chicken Run*, *Toy Story*, *The Incredibles* and *Monsters Inc*. However, digital animation is also widely used on a smaller scale to move logos and characters or objects on website pages. Adobe (Macromedia) Flash is widely used for creating digital animation in this field and can be used to produce short computer animation films as well.

PART 1: EXPLORE ANIMATION TECHNIQUES 2 Objective (1a)

Types of animation

Traditional animation techniques

Flipbook

A flipbook is a series of sketches that are usually hand drawn on each page of a small book, starting at the back and working towards the front. The book is then 'flicked' through to give a rapidly changing picture that gives the impression of movement.

Cel animation

In cel animation, each frame is produced from a number of cels. Each cel is produced on clear acetate film, so that only the parts of the frame that are moving need to be modified on the relevant cel. If the background is not moving, then the same background cel can be used for a number of frames, which reduces the amount of work involved.

Stop motion

This is a process of photographing physical objects that are moved slightly between each frame. By keeping the changes small each time, the effect of movement is created. Any objects can be used, for example moving a coin across a table or opening a bar of chocolate.

Modelling

Modelling animation uses clay, ColourClay or other types of plasticine. Small models of characters and objects are created by hand and photographed using stop motion. Larger models may have a wire framework to support the model, which also makes adjustments easier.

Cutout animation

This is another form of stop motion animation that uses cloth, paper, card or any other form of flat material. Graphics and images can also be created using a computer.

Time-lapse photography

This is similar to stop motion animation in that it uses a series of photographs. However, time lapse usually refers to objects that move naturally without being modelled by the animator. Examples would be a flower that opens up or a bird in flight.

PRACTICE EXERCISE

Experiment with clay modelling

1. Get some plasticine or clay and a basic set of plastic or wooden modelling tools that make it easier to shape and texture the clay.
2. Create characters or other objects with the clay.
3. Plan a short story using a basic storyboard.
4. Set up a camera in a fixed position and photograph the clay models, moving them slightly between each frame.
5. Copy the photographs to a computer to produce a short animation.

Note: If you don't have the tools and equipment for this, try creating a flipbook instead.

Computer/digital animation techniques

A computer can be used to create, digitize and/or edit a range of graphics, images and text. The process of creating a computer animation may involve several software applications. For instance, photographs may be processed in Adobe PhotoShop and vector graphics drawn in Adobe Illustrator. *Toy Story* was a full length CGI

(computer generated imagery) animation film produced by Pixar and released by Disney.

Computer animation software options

Adobe (Macromedia) Flash	Professional industry-standard software application that can be used to create anything from simple animated objects to short films.
Scratch	A freely downloadable application to produce animations and interactive media for use on the web.
CoffeeCup Firestarter	Open source application for basic animations.
Figure Stick®	A very basic program used to animate a simple 'stickman'. Can still be used to introduce the concepts of animation.

File formats and players for use with animation

Animation files can be created as:

- **gif:** Graphics interchange format, typically used for small animated objects on websites.
- **swf:** Originally Shockwave Flash Format but now known as just .swf it is commonly used for animated web graphics but requires the FlashPlayer plug-in to be installed (a free download from www.adobe.com).
- **HTML:** Can be used to produce animated files when saved and published with supporting files from Flash.
- **mov:** Apple Quicktime® movie format with players available for both PC and Apple Mac computers.

PRACTICE EXERCISE

Research uses and types of animation

1. Browse a range of websites and record what animation features are used.
2. Search on YouTube for animation.
3. Make a list of animation films.
4. Make a list of the uses for animation and the styles or types you have found. Your teacher may be able to help to identify what techniques were used in each case.

PART 2: PLANNING A DIGITAL ANIMATION

1 Objective (1a)

2 Objective (2a)

When planning your digital animation, you will need to consider the requirements of the client brief with the software that you have available. During the course delivery you may have developed an interest in a particular type of animation, whether it is stop motion, clay modelling or computer-based. Think about how to satisfy the needs of the client using your own creative talents, ideas and preferences for animation types. Because animation means the creation of moving images, a storyboard is almost essential as part of the planning process. Visualization diagrams and sketches can also be used to support the development of your ideas. Refer to the section on Planning and Review in the Introduction, which includes information on how to conceptualize, visualize and storyboard your work.

Of course you will need to document any use of copyrighted, trademarked or intellectual property. Keep records of all sources and permissions obtained for any material that is not your own.
Finally, think about how long the whole project will take. After your initial discussions with the client, they will want to know how long it will take to produce the work. Break this down into timescales for the creation of original assets, animation development and testing.

Creativity with digital animation

Think about what animation techniques you could use to create the final work. You could produce the assets that could be imported into the animation as part of the digital graphics/digital imaging unit. Compare and contrast the benefits and suitability of stop motion and clay modelling techniques with computer-generated images.
For both Level 1 and Level 2, this means developing a digital animation based on a storyboard that you will produce. The complexity of the animation and the tools used will be higher for Level 2 but the principles and processes are very similar.

Creating an animation storyboard

Storyboarding is used to show the progression of movement with time. It is an important part of the planning and development process for any moving image project.

frame 1	frame 2	frame 3	frame 4	frame 5	frame 6
●	●	●	●	●	●

This sequence of six frames will produce a bouncing ball effect when animated. If this was viewed at 12 frames per second (fps), the whole sequence would take 0.5 seconds from start to finish. The frame rate is an important part of the animation – if it is too low the movement will not be smooth or realistic. If it is unreasonably high then it will take a long time to produce because of the number of frames needed. The following table shows the total number of frames needed for an animation sequence at a range of frame rates.

	10 seconds	20 seconds	30 seconds	60 seconds
3 fps	30 frames	60 frames	90 frames	180 frames
6 fps	60 frames	120 frames	180 frames	360 frames
12 fps	120 frames	240 frames	360 frames	720 frames
24 fps	240 frames	480 frames	720 frames	1440 frames

If using stop-motion techniques, it soon becomes clear how much work is involved in creating feature-length animation films such as *Wallace and Gromit* or *Chicken Run*.

Identify what type of animation your work will take and what assets will be required. These may be digitized versions of traditional techniques or, alternatively, they could be created digitally.

PART 3: USING TOOLS AND FEATURES OF DIGITAL ANIMATION SOFTWARE

Using Adobe Flash

1 Objective (2a)

2 Objective (3a)

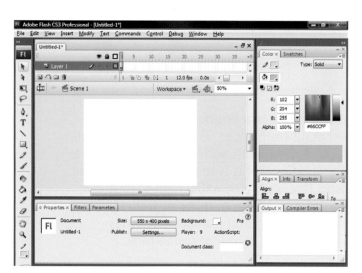

The Flash workspace

Some of the main features of the Flash workspace are:

- **Toolbox (Left):** A collection of tools for selection, drawing, and editing the assets imported to the stage.
- **Properties inspector (Bottom):** Used to define the properties of a selected object or asset.
- **Stage:** The central area where the graphical content of the animation is produced.
- **Timeline (Top):** Used to control how and when the objects or assets move during the animation sequence.
- **Panels (Right):** For managing library assets, alignment, colours and other features.

Introduction to digital animation using Flash

The process of creating an animation begins with creating or importing the assets. These are then animated on the timeline. The default frame rate in Flash is 12 frames per second (fps). So, for a two-second animation you will need a total of 24 frames. You do not necessarily have to create each frame but you must still define the content during playback of the animation.

Keyframes are those that signify a change to the animation, and they are literally the 'keys' to creating movement. In between keyframes, tweening can be used to fill in the positions and shapes of objects. Using this method, Flash will work out what happens to the object in between the first and last keyframe, whether it needs to change the shape or move it to a different position, hence creating the content of the frame for you. If stop-motion images are to be used in a frame-by-frame animation, then every frame will be a keyframe.

Working with symbols, instances and the library

In Flash, a symbol is defined from any single object or set of objects. These are stored in the library and each time a symbol is used in the animation, it is called an instance. One benefit is that the overall size of the file is minimised because it only has to store the symbol once.

Objects must be converted into symbols before they can be used on the stage in a motion or shape tween.

There are three types of symbols that can be created:

- **Movie clip:** this has its own timeline, which is different to the main timeline of the animation.
- **Button:** this is used when adding user interactivity to animation, e.g. click to start something or jump to a different page.
- **Graphic:** this is used with graphics that will be part of a simple animation, such as one you may produce for Levels 1 and 2.

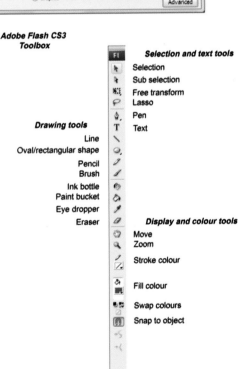

Adobe Flash CS3 Toolbox

Drawing tools
Line
Oval/rectangular shape
Pencil
Brush
Ink bottle
Paint bucket
Eye dropper
Eraser

Selection and text tools
Selection
Sub selection
Free transform
Lasso
Pen
Text

Display and colour tools
Move
Zoom

Stroke colour

Fill colour

Swap colours
Snap to object

Creating a basic animated object

In this example, we will look at how to create a simple banner for use on a website. This is not a comprehensive guide to using Adobe Flash but will cover the basic principles that are essential to meet the assessment objectives for the unit.

    From the 'File' menu, select 'New' (this can also be done from the start-up screen shown here). Choose ActionScript 3.0 (or use the latest version available in your own software).

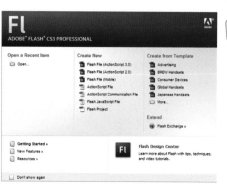

The Adobe Flash start-up screen

Set the size of the stage in pixels and the frame rate.

Import images/assets into the project

Select the 'File' menu > 'Import' > 'Image to stage'.

    Position the image on the stage. If the image has been prepared to the correct size, check that the X and Y coordinates (top left corner) are

The Layers/timeline panel

both 0.0 so that it fully covers the stage area. These coordinates can be found in the properties inspector.

Double-click on the Layer 1 name to give it a suitable name such as 'background'.

To make sure this background image is not moved when adding additional layers, lock it by clicking on the lock icon in the timeline alongside the layer name.

- Create a new layer and change the name to rain1.
- 'File' > 'Import' > 'Import to stage' *raindrop* image.
- Position the raindrop on the stage. From the 'Modify' menu, select 'Convert to symbol' (or press the F8 key). Choose a suitable name such as *rain_symbol* and the type 'Movie clip'. This conversion allows the image to be animated.
- Create a keyframe in frame 1 by pressing the F6 key. This function can also be found in the 'Insert' or 'Modify' > 'Timeline' menu.
- Create a second keyframe at frame 15. In the properties inspector, click on the 'Tween' option and select 'Motion'.
- Drag the background frame out to align with the end of the rain frames on the timeline.
- Create additional rain layers with raindrops in different positions so that the rain effect is constant when the animation is looped, i.e. replayed continuously.
- At any time, you can play the animation by pressing the 'Enter' key on the keyboard (or 'Control' menu > 'Play').
- A preview of the final animation can be seen by pressing F12 or selecting the 'File' menu > 'Publish Preview'.

Adding text

1 Objective (2b)

Create a new layer and rename it 'text' (or something suitable if there will be more than one text layer). Select the 'Text' tool in the toolbox and set the font/size/colour in the properties inspector. Click on the stage where you want to place the text and type the words using the keyboard. You can choose the 'Selection' tool from the toolbox to move or modify the text. You can also align the text to any part of the stage using the 'Align' panel. If this panel is not shown, select 'Window' menu > 'Align'. When complete, lock the text layer at the side of the timeline view.

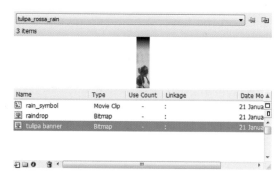

Working with the library

Items that have been imported to the stage will be shown in the library panel. After converting to a symbol, they can be dragged and dropped onto the stage as needed.

Animate the sequence

Objective (3b)

Flash provides the facility to tween movement between keyframes. As the animator, you decide the position of an object at a start point and end point on the timeline. These points are defined as the keyframes. Flash will then calculate the content for each

Flash timeline tween

frame 'in be*tween*' the keyframes to give a smooth transition of shape and/or motion.

In this example, we will animate the text layer with a motion tween. To start with, add keyframes in frame 1 and frame 40 by pressing F6 or selecting the 'Modify' menu > 'Timeline' > 'Convert to keyframes'.

In the properties inspector, select 'tween' > 'motion' between frame 1 and frame 40 to the text layer. At frame 1, the text is in the lower half of the stage. In frame 40, it has been positioned near the top of the stage. The motion tween calculates the position of the text for each frame in between. An alternative is a shape tween from the properties inspector, which modifies the overall shape of the object between the keyframes. After the tween has been applied, stretch the background layer out to frame 40 as well so it is always displayed during playback.

This is the final graphic that will be used on the web site. The animation has the raindrops falling constantly and can be found on the CD supplied with this book as both .fla and .swf files. The actual website can be found at: http://www.tuliparossa.com.

The final graphic

Tools and editing techniques

Frame-by-frame animation

With this type of animation the whole scene or stage is redrawn rather than a small part of it. The process of creating each new frame is made easier by using 'onion skinning' – or semi-transparent layers – to see what is behind. This means you can easily redraw a minor change or movement for the next frame in the sequence. This technique is quite advanced for Level 2 but you can still experiment with the possibilities.

Adding timeline effects

These are built-in animation effects that provide an easy way to create styles of movement and motion. You can choose from copy, blur, expand, explode, spin and fade in or out. To use an effect, first select an object on the stage. From the 'Insert' menu, select 'Timeline Effects'. The sub-menu options are 'Assistant', 'Effects' and 'Transform' with the following choices:

- **Assistant:** copy/duplicate
- **Effects:** blur, drop shadow, expand and explode
- **Transform:** transition (fade and wipe), transform (rotate, spin and change colour).

Note: To customise or remove the effect, select the 'Modify' menu > 'Timeline effects'.

Selection tools

The main selection tool is found at the top of the toolbox. With this tool, click on any item or object in the stage and the properties will be shown in the properties inspector. In the Tulipa Rossa banner, the text can be aligned to the centre of the banner from the 'Align' panel (if it is not shown, select the 'Window' menu > 'Align'). Make sure that 'To Stage' is enabled and use the alignment buttons to position the selected object. By using the 'To Stage' option, Flash will position the text with reference to the stage rather than other objects, for example, so that it is exactly in the middle of the stage (or banner in this example).

If you have several objects to be moved together, use the selection tool to click on each one while holding down the 'Shift' key. This allows multiple objects to be selected, all of which can then be moved or aligned as before. If the objects are to be animated together, you can also group them first from the 'Modify' menu > 'Group'.

Using drawing tools

In the Tulipa Rossa animated object, we looked at how to import images and animate them. Another way to produce the rain drops would be to draw them within Flash. The toolbox includes tools to draw lines, shapes and use fill colours. You can refer to the diagram with the list of tools in the drawing section to identify these in your own version of software.

In the example below, the sun was created with the oval tool. The yellow fill can be set with the fill colour tool or changed in the properties inspector afterwards. Gradient fill effects can also be used for more realistic 3D objects. The stroke setting in the properties inspector is used to create an outline around the object drawn, with options for both the stroke width and colour. The eraser tool is used to remove unwanted parts of any objects drawn. It works on all layers that are not locked. Use the lock icon to protect them from the eraser if needed.

The background sky and grass are on separate layers. The layers for the stick person and the 'Media' text are above the background layers (otherwise they would not be seen). The Flash file of this image is also supplied on the CD.

Both the pencil and brush tool have automatic smoothing of the edges. Use the selection tool to move, straighten or bend the lines and shapes drawn. Click and drag on any segment of the shapes.

Using stop motion with Flash animation

Flash can be used to produce an animation from photographs, for example, using stop-motion modelling or time-lapse photography. For the final work to be suitable for use on a website, the original photographs must first be processed in a digital graphics application. This is to resize them to a practical working size, such as 550 pixels wide × 400 pixels high, which is the default size of the stage. If each image is resized to 100KB and there are 20 images in the animation, the file will be at least 2MB (megabytes) in size unless further optimization is done.

To produce the animation, place the resized images on successive frames in the timeline. Titles in the form of text boxes can be added for the opening and closing credits. By using different layers on the timeline, you can start the stop-motion animation after the introduction section has completed.

Saving and exporting animation files

Objective (3b)

Objective (3c)

When saving files from Flash, they will have the file extension .fla, which keeps the structure of the layers and timeline intact. This format can only be viewed from within Flash and so for use on a web page or other computer, the file must be published. The recognised format for publishing is .swf. This is played using Adobe Flash Player, which is a free plug-in for a web browser. If your target computer does not have Flash Player, it can be freely downloaded from the Adobe website. Before publishing your work, check the publish settings from the 'File' menu – 'Publish settings'. The output formats that will be created are shown in a list, with detail tabs shown for each of the selected formats. If static (ie non-animated) images are required, choose the JPEG or PNG options.

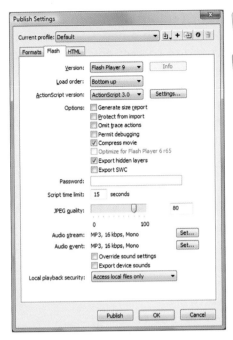

'Publish Options'

On the 'Flash' tab of the settings dialogue box, you will see the file settings that will be used. The version of Flash Player and ActionScript needed to play the file can be chosen along with the JPEG quality and audio stream. In general, leave these at the most recent (highest) versions available unless you really need to make it compatible with older versions. Lower values for JPEG quality and audio stream will reduce the size of file that is produced but check the quality of the final file that is created as a result. Comment on this aspect when you review your work.

Before publishing your animation, it is a good idea to

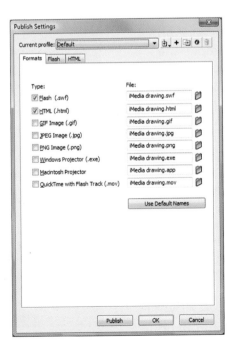

The Flash Publish screen

check that it works first using the 'Control' menu > 'Test Movie'. This will display your animation in a new window. If it does not display correctly, you will need to correct any problems found.

Once the settings have been configured, publish your animation from the 'File' menu > 'Publish'.

Examples of Flash animation files are supplied on the CD with this book. Have a look at the individual layers to identify what they do and how the animation is sequenced on the timeline with the keyframes.

Other software options for digital animation

Scratch

Scratch is available as a free download. It is a software application that can be used to create your own animations, interactive stories, games, music, and art. These can be saved in a format suitable for uploading to the web.

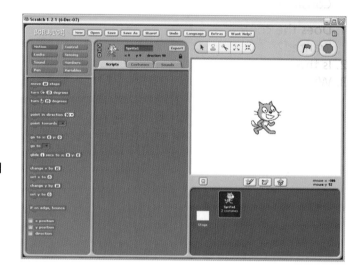

A series of blocks are provided to control the movement and actions of graphics and sprites imported. For example, the motion block enables movement of an object across the stage although there is no timeline as found in Flash.

CoffeeCup Firestarter®

With CoffeCup Firestarter you can combine text, graphics, images, sounds and shapes. They can be animated on a timeline with built-in motion effects. The cutting room panel uses layers for different objects or assets and the properties are displayed in the panel at the right-hand side.

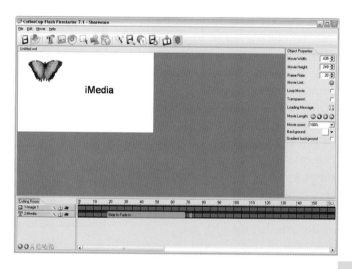

Files can be saved in .swf format for use on websites or used with the HTML code generator for publishing work.

PART 4: REVIEW YOUR ANIMATION

1 Objective (4a)

2 Objective (4a)

Your review of your digital animation needs to cover both the content and file size/format of the final work. The functionality testing of the animation should make sure that all aspects of the motion and movement work as expected and planned on the storyboard. Describe any significant changes to the plan and why these were made.

Consider the following questions:

1. Does the content of the animation show what the client actually wanted?
2. Is the total duration correct as requested by the client?
3. What is the final size of the animation file and is it suitable for use on a website?
4. What is the file format of the animation and what will be needed to view the file, e.g. Flash Player version 8/9/10?
5. Will the download speed be suitable on the expected Internet connection speeds?
6. Are the colour schemes suitable and any text easy to read?
7. Does the final work demonstrate a conventional or creative/innovative approach? There is no right or wrong here – just recognise what has been produced.
8. What improvements could be made? For example, frame rates, number of frames, animation techniques, colours, effects.

You may want to obtain some constructive comments from friends and the client in order to answer these questions. You could also refer to the general comments in the section on Planning and Review in the Introduction.

SUMMARY

By completing this unit you will have developed skills in producing an animation in response to a client brief. You will have produced an effective storyboard, used animation techniques and identified suitable file sizes and formats for use on websites. Great work!

FINAL ASSIGNMENT

Once you have learned all the required parts of the unit, you will complete an assignment that will be used to assess your knowledge and skills of the subject. It will be set in a vocational context, which means that it will simulate what it would be like to be given a project by a client or employer in a work situation. To start you should read the brief or scenario carefully to identify what is needed. A typical assignment may be in the following format (although these should not be used as templates for designing your own assignments – refer to the guidance documents on the OCR website for this purpose):

> *Brief:*
> *You are a junior animator for Tulipa Rossa sports goods and have been asked to develop a short animation on a sporting theme that could be used on their new website. For this you will need to produce a .swf file that lasts 20 seconds.*
> *Task 1: Here you may be asked to explore and experiment with a range of animation techniques that may be used to satisfy the brief.*
> *Task 2: In this task you will be asked to plan the development of your work. Use one or more of the planning methods described in the Introduction, identifying what you will need and how long it is likely to take. A storyboard would be a good approach for this since the animation will show movement along a timeline.*
> *Task 3: In this task you will be asked to actually produce or create your work. This should demonstrate a range of skills using the animation techniques and software. You will also need to test the finished animation to make sure it is suitable for use on a website (consider the file type and size).*
> *Task 4: In this task you should review your final work. This means thinking about things like overall quality, fitness for purpose and any areas for improvement. It is not just a summary of how you created the work – it should be a reflection by yourself (and others) on how suitable it is for use by the client described in the brief.*

Note that essential parts of the assignment include the planning and reviewing of your work. It is important to be able to think about what you need to produce and what the final work should look like. Since the assignment is in a vocational context it will be important to check the suitability of what you have produced before submitting it to the client. The development of these skills will be a great benefit when you are asked to produce something in the real/commercial world of employment.

Interactive Media

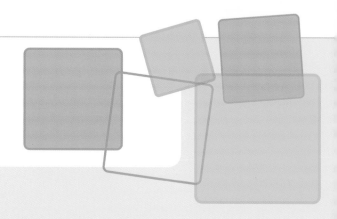

The aim of this unit is to create a multimedia product that enables the viewer to interact with the content. Multimedia by definition must have more than one type of media. It can include text, graphics, sound, video and animation. The interactivity means that the viewer has some control over the navigation, timing and/or information that is displayed. Because they can choose what is most relevant to them, it is more interesting for the viewer.

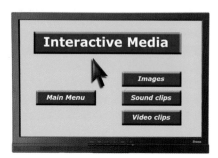

1 Unit 6

2 Unit 4

You will also find a summary of this unit on the CD supplied with this book as an interactive multimedia presentation. Try it if you would prefer to navigate through an audio-visual 'click and go' interface instead of reading this chapter.

For both Level 1 and Level 2, you will need to review the hardware, software and peripherals needed to develop and use interactive multimedia products. A range of assets may be sourced or created for use in your multimedia product, which will be enhanced by using interactive features. In some cases, you will be able to use your work from other chapters in this one. Good examples would be Chapter 2 Digital Graphics, Chapter 4 Digital Animation, Chapter 6 Digital Sound and Chapter 7 Digital Video.

PART 1: EXPLORE MULTIMEDIA TECHNOLOGY

2 Objective (1a)

Purpose: Where, when and why do we use interactive multimedia?

Effective multimedia products can be more interesting for the audience if they combine sound and visual effects because they stimulate the human senses of both hearing and vision. The addition of interaction also means that the user/audience is more engaged with the product and its content.

Because of this active participation by the viewer, interactive multimedia becomes more effective in areas such as:

- Education: The learning environment is more productive through active participation.
- Entertainment: Viewers can choose what they are interested in, so the content is more engaging and relevant to their needs.
- Advertising: The attention of the user is more focused on the product and its benefits.
- Information: A more specific focus on the information is provided that is directly relevant to the user's needs.

There are two main types of user for interactive multimedia products:

1. The actual end user/consumer, in which case the GUI (graphical user interface) must be very intuitive and easy to use.
2. Somebody who is presenting information to an audience. In this case the presenter decides on the timing and sequence of slides in response to the needs of the client and the audience, although there is no direct end user interaction.

> **PRACTICE EXERCISE**
>
> **Explore the use of multimedia**
>
> 1. Identify a range of places where multimedia products are used and the main purpose of them.
> 2. Test and explore the features of the multimedia products.
> 3. List what types of media are combined, e.g. text, graphics, sound, video, animation.
> 4. List what form of interactivity is included and consider how effectively it enhances the user's experience.
> 5. Summarise the best features of the multimedia product and consider how you could build these into your own work.

Hardware

You will need to consider both the hardware required to *produce* the multimedia product and the hardware needed to *use* or *view* the product.

Development platforms

Typically this will be a computer with suitable multimedia authoring software and peripheral devices. Both PC and Apple Mac computers can be used to develop and present multimedia, subject to the software available.

Software options for developing interactive media

Microsoft PowerPoint®	Commonly used for developing presentations for display to an audience
Adobe (Macromedia) Flash	Used to produce digital animation, which can be enhanced with multimedia and interactive buttons
Opus Presenter®	Dedicated multimedia presentation development software
Apple Keynote®	Part of the Apple iWork software suite
Adobe (Macromedia) Director®	Professional-level authoring tool for creating multimedia applications, games and simulations for CD/DVD, kiosks and the Internet

PRACTICE EXERCISE

Identify platforms and software available

1. List what computer platforms you have available in your centre.
2. Identify what software applications are installed and which could be suitable to support either the creation of assets or the authoring of multimedia presentations.
3. List the peripherals available, such as microphones, speakers, compact cameras, video cameras, web cameras, scanners, smart boards, etc.
4. Investigate a range of platforms and display devices that could be used to display or view the final work.

Viewing platform, systems and technology

Computers

This includes desktop, laptop and miniature notebook computers.

Display

Typical computer display monitors are between 15 and 20 inches wide, using either traditional CRT (cathode ray tube) or LCD (liquid crystal display) technology. Plasma display screens are usually around

42 inches wide and are used for larger audiences. Light projectors linked to a computer are used in larger rooms and halls.

Interactive features are also seen on television screens, especially with DVD movies or the latest Blu-Ray and HD-DVD formats.

Interactive whiteboards and smart boards

Using a projector connected to a computer, the user or presenter can interact directly with the smart board to control the presentation.

Mobile phones and PDAs

Larger colour screens on mobile phones allow more graphical user interfaces. Navigation arrow keys are used with selection and cancel/exit function buttons. A stylus is often used on touch- screen displays provided with a PDA.

Touch-screen displays

Kiosk displays often use touch-screen technology with unbreakable panels. This reduces the potential damage caused by vandalism and provides a direct and intuitive interface for the user who has not been trained in how to use the system. Another recent example of this type of interface is the Apple iTouch® and iPhone.

Websites

Websites can be developed using HTML or Flash. User-driven navigation combined with a wide range of content on demand mean that the Internet is a very capable platform for interactive media.

Peripherals (development and presentation/display)

Microphones

Microphones are used to record sounds and voiceovers to be used in the playback of the multimedia product. They can be attached directly to the computer or used as part of a separate sound recording device.

Speakers

Speakers are used to test the sound playback as well as present the final multimedia product. Headphones may also be used for testing purposes instead of speaker systems.

Wireless devices

Includes controllers and presentation aids so that the person delivering the multimedia presentation does not have to work directly on the computer.

Bluetooth connectivity can also be used with some devices. This is a short-range wireless communication system for transferring information and controlling other equipment. With any communication system, the bandwidth and limitations of the network speed must be considered. This is to ensure that the multimedia product does not take too long to load or play back to the audience.

Media players and plug-ins

Adobe Flash Player

This is Adobe's Flash player/viewer for .swf files. It is typically used in animation and provides support for interactive features.

Microsoft Windows® Media Player

This is Microsoft's viewer for a wide range of media and multimedia. It does not provide any options for interactivity other than play, pause, and so on.

Apple QuickTime®

This is Apple's viewer for movies created in QuickTime format. It does not provide any options for interactivity.

Sources of assets

Assets are defined as any image, graphic, sound clip, video clip, animation or even text that is to be used in your work. These assets are often imported into a library of your chosen multimedia authoring software. Some of these assets you can create yourself as original work. In this case, you will own the copyright on the asset. In other cases, you may source suitable assets from the World Wide Web or CD/DVD libraries and other discs.

   Some ways to create and/or source assets are shown in the following table.

Note: When sourcing any assets, consideration must be given to copyright, intellectual property and trademarks. You will need to reference this information and credit the author/owner where necessary.

Type of asset	Created by:	Sourced from:
Raster/bitmap images	• Using a digital camera to take photographs • Using a scanner on own images, graphics and drawings	• Scanning images and photographs • Web download • Image libraries • Client logo
Vector graphics	• Vector-based software such as Adobe PhotoShop and Illustrator	• Web download • Image libraries
Sound clip	• Recording own sounds and voiceovers using microphones and digital recording equipment	• Web download • CD/DVD • Sound effect libraries
Video clip	• Recording video footage using digital video camera, compact camera or suitable mobile phone	• Web download
Animation	• Animation and drawing software such as Adobe Flash, Scratch and FireStarter	• Web download
Text	• Writing own documents	• Your client • Web download • Wikipedia (most information is covered by the General Public Licence but do check this)

PART 2: PLANNING YOUR WORK

1 Objective (1c)

2 Objective (2a)

Read or discuss the client brief or specification carefully. Think about how to satisfy the needs of the client using your own creative talents and ideas. Note down some ideas on how to meet the needs of the client using good design principles. Part of your planning will overlap with your development of the interactive media product and structure. Discuss all of your ideas with the client before starting to develop the slides/pages. Visualization diagrams and sketches are one of the best ways to plan your work for this subject.

You will need to document any use of copyrighted, trademarked or intellectual property. Keep records of all sources and permissions obtained for any material that is not your own. You may also need model and/or property releases from people and property that may be identified in your work.

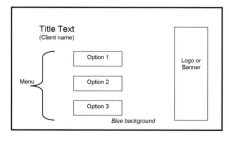

Finally, think about how long the whole project will take. After your initial discussions with the client, they will want to know how long it will take to produce the work. Break this down into timescales for sourcing assets, creating the media presentation and testing.

Design principles and content

2 Objective (2b)

There are three approaches to the design of interactive media products (although these also apply to many other subjects as well).

1. What the client wants
2. What the designer can do
3. What the user needs (considering the age and ability of the actual users).

Questions that you could ask yourself when you have completed the initial design include:

1. Will it look good?
2. Will it work?
3. Will it do what you want it to do?
4. Is it what the client wants?

When planning your work, take into account the following design considerations:

Target screen size

This affects the resolution of the graphics and video needed for the display screen. Higher resolutions will need larger file sizes and faster connections if being accessed over a network (e.g. the Internet). Touch screens may be used with larger screen sizes but small screens will most likely need to be controlled using function keys, keyboards or other interface devices.

GUI

This is the Graphical User Interface and covers the layout, colour schemes, navigation and interactivity. All of these factors will have an impact on the visual appeal, logical flow of information and the end user's experience of the multimedia interface.

Colour schemes

Pale backgrounds with dark text or dark backgrounds with light text will work best on a display screen. If a projector and screen is being used, there needs to be strong contrast between the text and background. Dark backgrounds with white text are often easier to read than pale backgrounds with black text when projected.

Font styles and sizes

Text should be easy to read, which means using a simple font style and size that is appropriate for the screen size and viewing distance.

User interaction features

These may include hyperlinks, buttons, rollovers and 'alt' text.

Navigation

Will this be menu-based or use links on text and graphics similar to a web page? Consider the purpose of your product and where it will be used before deciding what is most appropriate.

Background sounds or music

The choice of sounds and/or music should be appropriate for the message that is being presented. Sound volume levels and the mixing of voiceovers with background music should enable the listener to hear what is required clearly without having to replay it several times.

Accessibility

Accessibility is a term used to describe how easy it is for people with different abilities to access and use materials such as interactive multimedia and websites. In particular, the design should consider people with visual and hearing disabilities.

PART 3: CREATING MULTIMEDIA PRODUCTS

1 Objective (3a)

2 Objective (3b)

Adobe provides a range of software applications that can be used to develop interactive media solutions. However, this unit will begin by looking at the capabilities of Microsoft PowerPoint® to produce a multimedia presentation. Since Adobe Flash is also often used to create this type of product, the extra tools and techniques for interactivity in this program will be covered as well. Skip a few pages if you are already using Flash and need to know how to incorporate interactivity into your work.

Using Microsoft PowerPoint®

Start off creating a new project in Microsoft PowerPoint® by going to the 'File' menu > 'New'.

Formatting styles and layouts can be chosen from built-in themes. Select the 'Format' menu > 'Slide Design'. Click on any style to apply it to the presentation.

At the top of the slide design panel at the right-hand side, click on colour schemes. These can also be edited to use colours of your own choice from the 'Edit colour schemes' link at the bottom of the slide design panel.

To add a new slide, click on the 'New Slide' button on the toolbar. A range of pre-defined slide pages are available:

Importing assets

Objective (3b)

Insert/Import text

1. Create a text box using the 'Insert' menu > 'Text box'.
2. Click and drag the mouse to set the width of box required.
3. Either type in the words into the box or paste pre-copied text from other locations.
4. Format the text as required using the formatting toolbar or use the format menu for more options. This process is commonly used in a wide range of Microsoft applications.

Insert/Import pictures

Select the 'Insert' menu > 'Picture' > 'From File'.

Browse for the picture you want to insert and position it on the slide. The picture can be re-sized by dragging one of the corners in (or out) so that it is the correct size for the slide layout. Pictures that are to the optimum pixel dimensions and resolution should be produced and saved before being inserted (otherwise the file size of the final presentation could be too high).

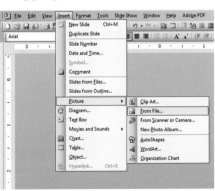

Insert/Import sound and video

1. Select the 'Insert' menu > 'Movies and Sounds' > 'Sound from File'.
2. Browse for the sound, video or movie file that is already stored on your computer system.
3. Using the 'Movies and Sounds' option, you can also record sound directly using a microphone connected to the computer. This could be in the form of a voiceover to introduce or explain parts of the multimedia presentation.

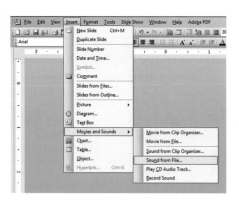

Once the sound has been inserted, right-click on the sound icon to edit the properties. If a background music track is being used, you can decide how playback should start and whether to loop the sound for continuous playing. Supported formats include aiff, au, midi, mp3, wav and wma.

Movie options can be set in the same way as sound files, by right-clicking with the mouse on the movie clip. Formats supported include mpeg, wmv, avi and asf.

Insert/Import animation

Animated objects can be inserted into Microsoft PowerPoint® in GIF file format. This is a type of image file rather than movie, so it is inserted in the same way as a picture. The animated movement will be seen when viewing the presentation using the 'Slide Show' menu > 'View Show'. This can also be tested using the 'Play' option on the slide animation control panel.

Add interactivity

Using Microsoft PowerPoint®, objects can be set to have hyperlinks and/or action settings attached to them. After inserting objects such as pictures and movies, right-click to set the interactivity options.

Using hyperlinks

Select any item on a slide, right-click with the mouse and then choose 'Hyperlink'. A link can be made to existing files/web pages, other slides in the same presentation or to a contact email address. The navigation link can be enhanced using a 'ScreenTip', which will be displayed when the mouse is moved over the object. You can edit the hyperlink settings at any time by right-clicking on the object and selecting edit (or remove) hyperlink.

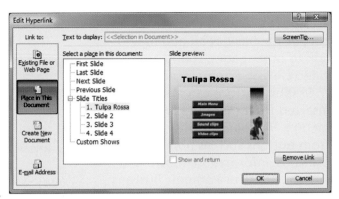

Using action settings

Select any item on a slide and right-click with the mouse. Select 'Action Settings'. The two tabs provide options for actions based on a mouse 'click' or just positioning the mouse cursor 'over' the object. The choice of actions includes hyperlinks, running new programs or playing sound/video files.

Rollovers

From the 'Action Settings' a rollover is created using the 'Mouse Over' tab. Options are available to add hyperlinks, run programs, play sounds or just highlight the object. If creating a hyperlink, you can enter or paste the full URL (e.g. a web address) into the URL field box.

Buttons

Buttons for navigation and actions in the multimedia product can be

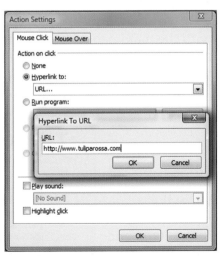

Adding a hyperlink using Action Settings

created using a digital graphics software application or imported as clip art. They are often used as part of the navigation and may link to other pages, sound and video clips or external websites.

Graphic buttons can also be inserted from the 'Slide Show' menu > 'Actions Buttons'. Choose from buttons such as home, next, previous, information, movie and custom. These are graphic buttons that are placed on the slides using the mouse to click and drag to the required size. A dialogue box for the properties for the action button will be displayed.

Add navigation

For Level 1, navigation through the multimedia product could be a simple linear progression from one page to the next using buttons and links. At Level 2, it is expected that a non-linear multimedia product will be created. This means that the user will be able to navigate across pages to different sections at will. Use a method of being able to go straight back to the main menu (home page) on each slide.

The image below shows the main screen for a Tulipa Rossa multimedia presentation. The buttons were created using Adobe PhotoShop as a coloured box with a bevel and emboss layer style. Text was added for each of the buttons, which were saved as JPEG files for insertion onto the main page/slide. A hyperlink was added in Microsoft PowerPoint® to create the navigation through to the appropriate slide or other location.

Enhance the multimedia project

Using slide transitions

Transitions control how the change occurs between each slide. Options include dissolve, fade and wipe schemes. The transition can be set for individual slides or the

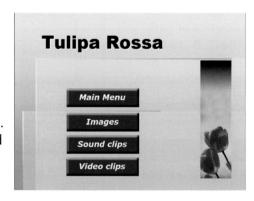

entire slide show. Sound effects and the speed of the transitions can also be modified.

Using animation schemes

Microsoft PowerPoint® provides a range of animation schemes that control the way in which objects and information on each slide is displayed. These can be found in 'Slide design' > 'Animation schemes'.

In addition to the standard animation schemes, a custom scheme can be created. This allows you to add effects to each item or object on the page. The effects are chosen from entrance, emphasis, exit and motion paths. Multiple effects can also be setup and a preview checked by clicking on the 'Play' button.

Adding alternative text

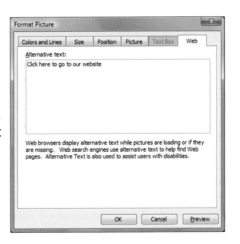

Web browsers support the display of alternative (or 'alt') text information. This is displayed whenever the mouse is held over the object. To add alternative text, right-click on the image or graphic and select 'Format picture'. The text information is entered on the Web tab. Note that this is only displayed when the multimedia product is saved in HTML format and viewed in a web browser.

Publishing a multimedia product

The final file size will depend on the file size of images, graphics, sounds and movies that have been used. Ideally these will have been prepared in suitable resolutions and file formats before being inserted into the multimedia product. If not, Microsoft PowerPoint® has some options for optimization prior to publishing. For example, images can be compressed by right-clicking on one of the images and selecting 'Format Picture'. On the 'Picture' tab, there is an option to 'Compress', which will provide options for web/screen or print resolution of images. Apply the required setting to all images in the presentation.

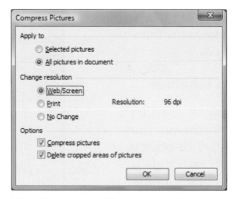

Formats available from Microsoft PowerPoint® include:

The Compress Pictures option

- **PowerPoint File:** This is a standard .ppt file format used by Microsoft PowerPoint®. This is used to save the files when developing the multimedia product but alternative formats are needed for publishing purposes unless the target platform also has Microsoft PowerPoint® installed.
- **PowerPoint Show:** This is suitable for use and presentation on another computer with a .pps file extension (requires a Microsoft PowerPoint® player/viewer).
- **HTML:** This is a standard format that can be viewed on any computer with a web browser. Note that the presentation pages will need to be zipped into a single file for uploading to the e-Portfolio for your final assignment.
- **Package for CD:** This can be used when publishing the presentation to a CD or DVD. Options can be included to provide the Microsoft PowerPoint® viewer in addition to the files for playback. Using this option will make sure that all the necessary files, such as embedded movies will work during the playback.

A presentation can be saved in image file formats such as JPEG, PNG and GIF. Note that these export each slide as a separate image file and the interactivity will not work. Because of this, they are NOT suitable formats for publishing work in this unit.
In all cases, the filenames chosen should be descriptive of the content.

2 Objective (3d)

Testing the interactive media presentation

Functionality testing is completed to make sure the interactive media presentation works as expected. The main two parts you need to check are the navigation and page/slide display.

The main purpose of navigation testing is to make sure that all pages/slides are accessible and there are no incorrect links and inaccessible pages. A good approach is to view the published presentation and check every navigation button and hyperlink as if you were the end user.

Creating a test plan

Functional testing is completed by producing a test plan first, which lists the tests to be run and provides space for the results to be noted down.

Test plan			
Test	Criteria for pass/fail	Pass/fail result	Comments
Main menu slide buttons and links	All buttons and links working	√	Internal and external OK
Main menu slide graphics display	Images and graphics correct size and position	√	
Main menu page/text layout HTML version	Check in a range of browsers	√	Using IE7 and Firefox
Sound and video playback	Autostart on sound, mouse click on video to start	√	
Continued. . .			

Other software options for creating interactive media

Using Adobe Flash

Flash can be used to create interactive multimedia presentations by adding action buttons. A good approach is to develop presentations with multiple scenes, where each scene is a new slide (or page). In the previous chapter on animation, you will have most likely created animated objects using the timeline in a single scene.

To create a new scene, select the 'Insert' menu > 'Scene'. Create the contents for each scene by importing, creating and/or drawing the objects required (see Chapter 4 for more information on how to do this is Flash). Once created, use the scene selection icon at the top right of the workspace window:

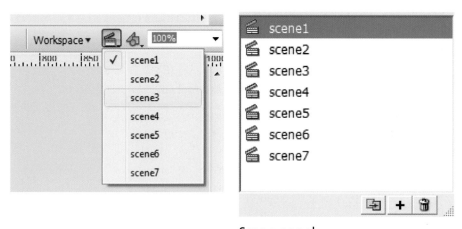

Scene panel

You can manage the scenes from the 'Window' menu > 'Other panels' > 'Scene'. This allows you to delete, duplicate or add new scenes.

Navigation between scenes can be achieved by creating 'buttons' and applying 'actions'.

Having created the scenes, navigation and user interaction can be added by using buttons with action script applied to them.

There are two main types of buttons that can be used for user interaction:

Visible

This is a button that clearly identifies what will happen when the user clicks on it. It may have a title of 'Next page' or 'Continue' for example. A series of visible buttons could also be created as a main menu.

Invisible

This type of button is not seen on the stage but can be used to detect when the user clicks anywhere inside it. Invisible buttons should not be too small and may cover the entire area of the stage.

To create an invisible button:

1. Create a new layer and rename it 'button'.
2. Use the drawing tools to create a shape area on the stage without an outline stroke colour.
3. Select the shape using the selection tool and modify the size and position if needed in the property inspector. The transform tool can also be used for this.
4. Convert the shape to a symbol (either right-click, use the 'Modify' menu > 'Convert to symbol' or press F8). Choose a name for the symbol such as 'invisible button'.
5. Double-click the button on the stage to change to the symbol editing mode. Notice that the timeline view changes to up, over, down and hit options. These are used to define what the button looks like to start with and how it changes when the user moves or clicks with the mouse on it. To create an invisible button, only the 'hit' frame is needed, so drag the rectangle across to this frame. If visible buttons are being created, you will need to define the up, over and down frames as well.
6. When complete, click in the scene 1 icon to exit the symbol editing mode.

Before adding any 'action' code to the button, it must first be converted to an instance so that it can be recognized from the timeline. To do this, select the 'invisible button' on the stage and type 'next_btn' into the instance name field in the properties inspector. Insert a new layer on the timeline and rename it 'actions'.

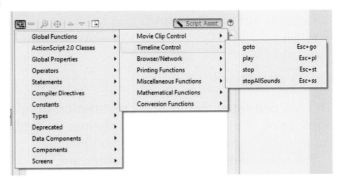

The 'Actions' panel is used to create or define the script for each button in the scene. You can find it under the 'Window' menu >'Actions' (or press F9 on the keyboard).

```
on (release) {gotoAndPlay("scene2", 1);
```

Using the example of a 'Next' button, an example of the script to go to the next scene on release of the mouse key is shown (above):

You need to define each button in the interactive media presentation in a similar way to enable navigation between scenes and the playing of media clips. Develop a test plan for the interactive media product as detailed earlier in this chapter.

Using Apple Keynote on a Mac Computer

As part of the iWork suite there is an application called Keynote. This is similar to Microsoft PowerPoint® in that it is a software application for producing presentations.

The main features of Apple Keynote are:

- Slide layouts can be chosen from a range of built-in themes.
- Text, media, tables and charts can be inserted on slide pages using the shortcut icons at the top of the screen.
- The inspector icon is used to set the properties for objects inserted on the slide pages. In this example a hyperlink is being added to the right arrow for a different slide in the presentation.
- There is a limited range of enhancement effects. Suitable export formats with interactivity features include Flash, iDVD and HTML.

Opus Presenter

This is a dedicated multimedia presentation development software application. It provides a range of themes, including one specifically for interactive presentations and multimedia.

The main features of Opus Presenter are:

- Templates are included for interactive presentations, menus, rolling demos and training.
- It has the ability to auto-scale the publication for any screen size.
- There is a wide range of page content layouts.
- Tabs for objects, actions and resources are included.
- Resources are built in for interactive features such as rollovers, animation, multiple-choice questions, text input boxes, hot spots and frames.
- Options are provided for publishing as a standalone or web format, in addition to saving in the generic .imp format.

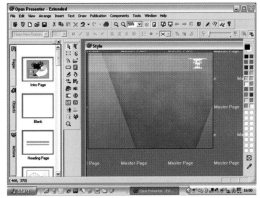

PART 4: REVIEWING YOUR WORK

1 Objective (4a)

2 Objective (4a)

The review of an interactive multimedia presentation is the final stage after the functional testing. This should cover basic design principles and the needs of the client and target audience. Consider the following questions:

1. Does the content of the presentation show what the client actually wanted?
2. Are the text and graphics a suitable size for the client and target audience?
3. Is the download speed appropriate for the expected Internet connection speeds?
4. Is the colour scheme visually pleasing and easy to read? For example, is there good contrast between the text and background colour?
5. Does the final work demonstrate a conventional or creative/innovative approach? There is no right or wrong here – just recognise what has been produced.
6. What improvements could be made? For example in colours, layout or navigation.

You may want to obtain some constructive comments from friends and the client in order to answer these questions. You could also refer to the general comments in the the section on Planning and Review in the Introduction.

SUMMARY

By completing this unit you will have developed skills in producing an interactive multimedia product in response to a client brief. You will have identified suitable hardware and software for development, display and user interactivity. Having combined a range of text, graphics, sound and video, you will have been able to test the functionality and review the layout and colour schemes to make sure the multimedia product meets the needs of the client and target audience.

FINAL ASSIGNMENT

Once you have learned all the required parts of the unit, you will complete an assignment that will be used to assess your knowledge and skills of the subject. It will be set in a vocational context, which means that it will simulate what it would be like to be given a project by a client or employer in a work situation. To start you should read the brief or scenario carefully to identify what is needed. A typical assignment may be in the following format (although these should not be used as templates for designing your own assignments – refer to the guidance documents on the OCR website for this purpose):

> *Brief:*
> *You are a junior media designer for Tulipa Rossa sports goods and have been asked to develop a multimedia presentation for a new range of sports goods. The presentation should be 4–6 pages and allow the user to control the movement between the pages using a range of interactive features.*
> *Task 1: Here you may be asked to explore the features, benefits and application for interactive media products.*
> *Task 2: In this task you will be asked to plan the development of your work. Use one or more of the planning methods described in the Introduction, identifying what you will need and how long it is likely to take. The layout of sample pages should be shown using a visualization diagram or sketch, which also identifies how the user will interact with it.*
> *Task 3: In this task you will be asked to actually produce or create your work. This should demonstrate a range of skills*

using the multimedia authoring software. You will also need to test the finished product to make sure the interactivity, navigation and text/graphics work correctly.

Task 4: In this task you should review your final work. This means thinking about things like overall quality, fitness for purpose and any areas for improvement. It is not just a summary of how you created the work – it should be a reflection by yourself (and others) on how suitable it is for use by the client described in the brief.

Note that essential parts of the assignment include the planning and reviewing of your work. It is important to be able to think about what you need to produce and what the final work should look like. Since the assignment is in a vocational context it will be important to check the suitability of what you have produced before submitting it to the client. The development of these skills will be a great benefit when you are asked to produce something in the real/commercial world of employment.

Digital Sound

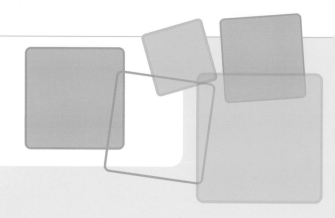

The aim of this unit is to learn how to record and edit a range of digital sounds. It covers how and where sound is used, together with equipment and software applications for recording and editing. You will learn how to record different types of sound and combine these to produce a range of new digital sound files.

2 Unit 5

2 Objective (1a)

Where, when and how sound is used

Sound may take the form of voiceovers, background music, event/actions or vox pop. These can be used in radio, television, broadcasting, websites, games or computer sounds for events such as start-up. Some examples are:

- **Broadcasting:** Radio and television often use voiceovers, jingles and adverts.
- **Web:** Some websites incorporate sounds such as background music, voiceovers or page clicks.
- **Multimedia:** Any type of multimedia product or presentation can also use sounds to enhance the experience. It may also include ring tones on mobile devices.
- **Games:** Sound is often used for background music, environment sounds (e.g. water, animals) or actions/events.
- **Computer sounds:** Sound can be used for start-up, shutdown, error messages, alerts and alarms.

PART 1: TECHNOLOGY USED TO RECORD AND PRODUCE DIGITAL SOUND

> ## PRACTICE EXERCISE
>
> **Research and review the use of sound**
>
> 1. Make a list of where sounds are used, e.g. radio, television, games.
> 2. Identify why each sound is used and what is the main purpose.
> 3. Note down the main characteristics such as duration, tone, content (e.g. mixed music and voice).
> 4. Think about how you might go about creating something similar.

Quality considerations

The quality of sound will be dependent on a number of factors such as:

- equipment used to record the sound
- settings used for recording (e.g. sample rate, bit depth)
- volume levels and background noise
- file format used to save the sound
- equipment used to playback the sound

There are a number of factors that can be used to describe the quality of sound. These are:

Volume

The volume refers to the sound level and a higher volume means a louder or higher signal level. It is used for both the recording and playback of sounds. During playback, the volume (or loudness) must allow the listener to hear the sounds clearly. However, the human ear does not have the same sensitivity to all frequencies of sound, which is why some sounds can appear louder even though they are at the same volume level.

Signal-to-noise ratio (SNR)

This is the ratio of the sound signal compared to that of any noise and is usually expressed in dB (decibels). A SNR of 10dB means the signal is ten times the value of the noise (10:1), which would be very poor; 20dB is a ratio of 100:1 and 30dB is a ratio of 1000:1, which is a more realistic minimum value. Note that increasing the volume (or amplification) of a sound will increase *both* the signal and the noise, hence the SNR will stay the same.

Tone

Tone can be described as 'any sound with a definite pitch' or 'a single note without overtones'.

Pitch

Pitch can be described as 'the perceived fundamental frequency of a sound – which may have a number of overtones or harmonics'.

Timbre

This is the quality or character of the sound that distinguishes it from something similar. Timbre can also be described as the tonal colour of the sound, which can be warm or cold. An example would be the same musical note played on a piano or violin.

Clarity

This is how pure or clear the sound is. When listening to a person's voice – how easy is it to make out what they are saying?

Interference

Interference is when two or more signals combine with each other to degrade or lower the quality of the desired sound signal.

Balance

This is a term used to describe the ratio of the volume levels between the left and right channels of a stereo sound.

Digital sound recording

2 Objective (1b)

Digital recording devices take thousands of samples per second of the amplitude (volume) from a microphone. This is achieved using analogue to digital converters (ADC). If the sampling rate is fast enough, the digital sound data will be an accurate copy of the original analogue sound waveform.

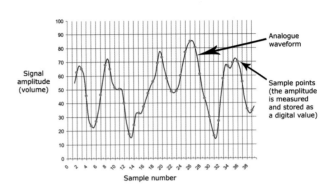

One major benefit of digital sounds is that they can be copied without any loss of quality. This is not the same as analogue recordings, because tape-to-tape copies will result in some loss of detail or quality. Sound editing is also much easier when using digital sound, in the same way as video editing.

The human ear can detect sounds in the range of 20 Hz to 20 kHz. Many telephone systems still work using a bandwidth of 300 Hz to 3 kHz, cutting off the higher frequencies between 3 kHz and 20 kHz. This is why people sound a bit different on the telephone, although this bandwidth is good enough for conversational use.

Sample rates and bit depth

Audio CDs contain sound that has been sampled at 44.1 kHz, which means that there are 44,100 samples for every second.

Note: 1 Hz = 1 hertz = 1 sample per second
1 kHz = 1 kilohertz (1000 Hz)

Digital sound is usually recorded at either 12-bit or 16-bit quality settings. For the purposes of sound recording in this unit, a 16-bit depth can be considered to give a more detailed and accurate recording of the volume levels whereas 12-bit produces good quality with smaller file sizes.

There is a difference between audio level compression and audio file compression. Audio level compression is used to reduce the dynamic range, that is, the difference between the loud and quiet parts. Audio file compression represents the use of encoding to reduce the size of the file for transmission, such as with mp3. The use of audio file compression through the file format, will determine the size of the file that is produced as your final work. Not all audio project work needs to be of CD quality but you need to know when something less than this will be good enough for the end user and how far you can go before it is completely unsuitable.

Sound file formats

Digital sound file formats

There are two main categories of sound file – compressed and uncompressed. The main file types or formats are listed below:

Uncompressed file formats using Pulse Code Modulation (PCM)	
WAV	Windows Wave Format, which is widely supported by computer systems and web browsers
AIFF	Audio Interchange File Format, the default audio format used on Apple Mac computers

Compressed file formats	
mp3	MPEG-1 audio layer 3, an audio format that can be compressed using different bit rates, providing a range of options for the sound quality/file size
WMA	Windows Media Audio format developed by Microsoft
Ogg Vorbis	Alternative to mp3 with similar file sizes
AAC	Advanced Audio Coding format, based on MPEG-4 and used by Apple
AU	Audio file format developed by Sun Microsystems for use with Unix and Java

Computer hardware

Either a PC or Mac with a sound card can be used for sound projects.

Internal sound cards

Have a look at your computer system to identify whether it has a sound card fitted. You can look for the microphone and speaker sockets described later in this section.

Plug-in sound cards can be fitted to a desktop PC using the PCI bus and are available with different specifications. The PCI bus provides expansion card slots

An internal sound card

for sound, video and communication cards. Once fitted, the connections for the sound card are available at the rear of the computer although sometimes they are also available on the front for ease of access. A sound card will have analogue to digital conversion (ADC) for recording sound, and digital to analogue conversion (DAC) for playing sound back through speakers. More advanced sound cards provide surround sound capability, which can drive six or more speakers.

Sound card specifications

Feature	Minimum	High performance
Bit depth (recording)	16-bit	24-bit
Sampling speed (recording)	44.1kHz	96kHz or 192kHz
SNR	90dB	100dB+
Playback	16-bit, 44.1kHz	24-bit, 192kHz
Sockets	Microphone	Microphone
	Headphones	Line in
		Digital out
		Headphones
		5.1 Surround sound
		• Front left/right
		• Centre/subwoofer
		• Surround left/right

Connections are usually colour coded 3.5mm sockets:

- **Blue:** line in (from external sources such as audio playback devices)
- **Green:** speakers
- **Pink:** microphone.

External sound cards

These will connect to the computer or laptop by either USB or FireWire ports. They minimise any potential problems with internal electrical noise from electronics in the computer.

Another example of external sound capture is the Rode Podcaster. This is a broadcast-quality microphone that connects by USB to any computer. The analogue to digital conversion (ADC) is built in to the microphone itself.

Sound and audio device properties

Handheld digital sound recorder

In the Microsoft Windows® Control panel you will find the sounds and audio devices. These settings may be used control the recording and playback volume when recording sound directly into Microsoft Office® applications for example. However, in this unit you will be using dedicated recording software to capture the sounds, which have their own recording controls.

Storage of sound recordings

Analogue tape

This can be convenient for the initial recording using a portable device, but the sound will still need to be digitized for use in editing software on the computer.

Digital formats

Digital sound recordings can be stored on the computer hard disk, CD, DVD, mp3 player, flash memory devices, external hard disks or even mobile phones. They can also be transmitted over the Internet very easily. The size of the digital file will be dependent on the format used. This is an important consideration for applications such as games, where most of the available memory and computer processing power is used to render the 3D graphics.

Recording equipment and peripheral devices

Microphones

The purpose of a microphone is to convert sound into electrical signals that can be digitized on the sound card by the computer. There are several different types:

Dynamic

Dynamic microphones range from economical general purpose microphones through to professional vocal types (recognised by their lower impedance). They do not have the same flat-frequency response of condenser types and don't need power because they do not have an internal amplifier.

Condenser

A condenser is a microphone that uses a capacitor (condenser) to respond to the sound level and converts this to electrical signals.

Unlike a dynamic microphone, it needs power to operate either from an internal battery or external 'phantom' power source. Many external video microphones are condenser types and may have XLR-type connectors instead of the smaller 3.5mm jack.

Electret

Electret is a type of condenser microphone with built-in supply voltage for the capacitor. Hence it does not require an external phantom power source.

Lavalier

A lavalier is a small lapel or tie-clip condenser microphone used to pick up the speech from one person, in an interview for example.

Characteristics of microphones

Directionality

Directionality refers to the direction where the microphone is sensitive to sounds. All microphones will pick up sounds from directly in front but some are not as sensitive to sounds from the sides. This property is usually illustrated using a polar pattern diagram as shown (right).

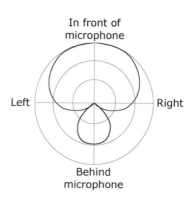

Omni-directional

This microphone picks up sound from all directions, that is, equally in front of the microphone and behind.

Cardioid

Cardioid is a word that usually refers to the heart – and in microphone terms this means a heart-shaped polar pattern. The strongest signal comes from sounds that are directly in front of the microphone with almost nothing from behind.

Omni-directional

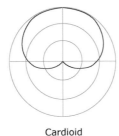
Cardioid

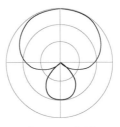
Super-cardioid

Super-cardioid

Super-cardioid is a narrow directional microphone useful for picking up sounds with a specific source or at a longer distance, for example wildlife or from a stage.

Shotgun

A shotgun microphone has a very narrow forward pointing response although it may also have a significant sensitivity to sounds directly behind it as well.

Some video microphones have a variable zoom or directionality control. This can be useful for different types of shots and footage recording. When using this type of microphone, it is best to setup the zoom control first and not change it during the actual recording.

Impedance

Low impedance microphones tend to give higher-quality results (<600 ohms). High impedance microphones (>10,000 ohms) can be quite cheap but the recording will be more likely to be affected by background electrical noise. In this situation the SNR of the recording could be quite poor.

Frequency response

This describes how the microphone responds to the sound. Some microphones are more sensitive to higher or lower frequencies, for instance. A flat response gives the most natural recording but is not necessarily the best. If you want to record a person's voice in an environment with a low-frequency background noise, a microphone that is not as sensitive to low frequencies would be better.

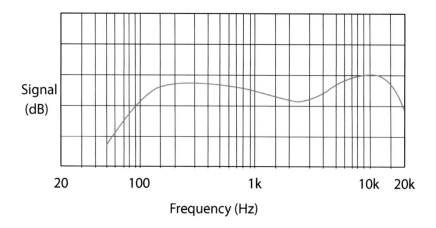

Accessories

Line amps

Line amps boost the signal from a microphone; they are often used with dynamic types of microphone.

Sound mixers

These may have inputs for several microphones and volume controls (using amplifiers) to match the signal level from each microphone. An example would be the Folio Notepad. This is more of an analogue technique but it is still important to have a strong signal before sampling and saving, otherwise the SNR may still be poor. The mixing can also be done within a sound editor program (covered later in this chapter).

Dead cat

The dead cat is a furry wind shield to minimise the sound of the wind on the microphone.

Shock mount holder

This is sometimes used to suspend the microphone with elastic to eliminate handling and movement sounds.

Boom arm and/or stand

These hold the microphone steady and in the correct position for the recording.

Phantom power supplies

These are for use with condenser microphones when other power sources are not available.

Hand-held recorders and other devices

Apart from microphone and computer systems, there is a range of other recording equipment that can be used:

- dictation machines (analogue tape or digital)
- mini disks
- mobile phones (using the voice memo feature)
- video cameras (can leave the lens cap on and just record the audio using a suitable microphone).

Speakers

These are the opposite of microphones but have a very similar construction. The purpose of a speaker is to convert electrical signals into sound that can be heard.

Standard computer speakers (or built into laptop)

Sound quality varies between computers – some are designed for high-quality multimedia and may have high-quality stereo sound systems. Other models may have a very basic mono speaker.

External amplifier and speakers

The standard headphone socket will not drive high-powered speakers and needs external amplification to drive larger speakers. You can purchase speaker systems that have their own separate mains power supply and still connect to the standard headphone socket. More advanced (expensive) sound cards have specific outputs for 'surround sound' speaker systems, as mentioned earlier.

PART 2: PLANNING YOUR WORK

Before planning the recording of your sounds, you will still need to know what is required for the sound project. This will be described in a client brief or specification. Read this document carefully and think about how to satisfy the needs of the client using your own creative talents and ideas. Note down some ideas on how to complete the sound recording and what equipment will be needed.

Discuss all of your ideas with the client before going out to record the actual sounds. Storyboarding is not necessarily going to be the best way to plan your work for this subject. You will certainly need an equipment list and probably a concept of what will be created that can be shown to your client. If you are developing initial ideas, try a spider diagram and see what you come up with. This is described in more detail in the Planning and Review section of the Introduction, if you are not sure about what needs to be included.

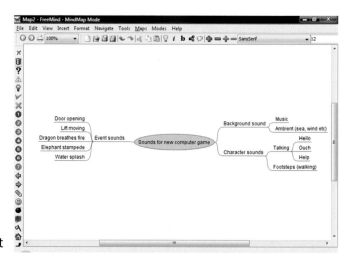

Of course you will need to document any use of copyrighted, trademarked or intellectual property. Examples would be sound or music files which may not be copyright free. Keep records of all sources and permissions obtained for any material that is not your own using the form provided on the CD (or an equivalent).

Finally, think about how long the whole project will take. After your initial discussions with the client, they will want to know how long it will take to produce the work. Break this down into timescales for the recording and editing of sounds.

PART 3: HOW TO RECORD, SOURCE AND EDIT DIGITAL SOUND

2 Objective (3a)

Recording sound

An important part of preparation is deciding what equipment to use. This includes the choice and characteristics of microphones, recording equipment and sampling rates. Find out what the options are for using an outside location or if the recording could be completed in a sound studio. If you are working in a sound studio it will be much easier to control the background noise and interference. If working outside, think about how best to control background sound, for example the time of day, road noise, ticking clocks, computer noise, fans and other people. Check the sample rate, bit depth and other settings on hardware devices such as a video camera if one is being used.

How to choose the right microphone

Think about the directionality and frequency response. Review the types and characteristics of the microphones described earlier. Examples would be:

- hand-held omni-directional dynamic
- cardioid or super-cardioid condenser
- lavalier.

By using the most appropriate type of microphone, you will increase the chances of a high-quality recording.

Considerations when setting up a microphone

- **Distance:** Set for the best sound signal-to-noise ratio (but not too close so as to get distortion).
- **Recording levels:** Check before recording the actual sounds needed.
- **Microphone handling and wind noise:** Use shock mount holders and/or a 'dead cat'.

If you are recording a voice interview, maintain a constant distance between the mouth and the microphone to keep the recording volume at a constant level. Try to avoid the idea that you can fix it in the sound editor later – it will take a lot longer and the results are unlikely to be as good as a first-class recording. Use the pointing of the microphone as a cue for who should be speaking.

   Note: a directional microphone (especially shotgun types) should be pointed at the mouth of the person, not just the body. Moving 'off target' with this type of microphone can affect the recording volume quite easily. Refer to the polar diagram of the microphone to see where the sensitivity starts to drops away.

Choice of sampling rates

A good starting point for sampling rates and bit depth would be 44.1kHz and 16 bits as described at the beginning of this chapter. If using a digital video camera, most will also have a 12-bit option to keep the size of audio tracks smaller, so check the settings in the menu. If editing, mixing and effects are to be added, it is better to start with high-quality recordings then save the sound in one of the compressed formats to reduce the size of the final work.

Sourcing digital sound files

In addition to recording sounds, you may be able to source these from pre-recorded locations, although you must check any copyright issues.

Sources of sound

- **Web:** sounds available from the Web are usually available in mp3 format.
- **CD/DVD:** Music and sounds can be 'ripped' from the discs but you must be aware of any copyright restrictions. Look for CDs created that specifically state that they are copyright free for use in video projects or 'music on hold' telephone systems.
- **Sound library:** Licensing fees and usage rights must be checked and observed when sourcing sounds from these commercial libraries.

Digital sound files may be obtained in a range of file formats. Many of these should be supported by your sound editing software, although you need to be aware of the sound quality that can be achieved when using compressed formats.

Software options

2 Objective (3b)

Some of the software options are:

Name	Provider	Description
Audacity	Soundforge	A widely used open source sound editor with a good range of tools and features.
Audition®	Adobe	A professional sound editing application for sound designers, mastering engineers and musicians.
Soundbooth®	Adobe	Integrated with other Adobe Creative Suite 3 products for creative professionals and developers with an easy to use task-based interface.
Garageband®	Apple	A well-featured sound editing application for the Apple Mac and part of the iLife software suite.

Basic sound editing can also be completed in many video editing software applications, but you will need to check what formats the sound can be saved in.

Editing digital sound

In this section you will learn how to use digital sound software to import, edit, combine and produce new sound files.

Creating digital sound can be split into two main sections: the original recording and post processing of the digital sound files. The post processing can be further split into two parts: the cleaning up of the original sounds followed by the creation of new sound tracks for project or assignment work. The techniques involved in these two post-processing activities are shown below:

1. Clean up recordings:
   a. trim, cut and copy selections from tracks
   b. volume/gain adjust
   c. noise removal
   d. save as new files in an uncompressed file format.
2. Mixing audio tracks and adding effects:
   a. import audio tracks required for project or assignment work
   b. mix ambient sound tracks with vocals or other content

c. align sound tracks or synchronise with video

d. add effects for fade in/out, reverb, mono/stereo conversion

e. audio level compression

f. exporting and saving.

Audacity user interface

This is a freely available, open source sound-editor program. It can be used for recording and editing digital sounds. As it is available as open source software, new revisions are constantly being developed and made available for free download under the GNU General Public Licence (GPL).

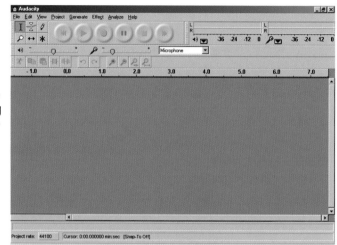

Note that the project sampling rate is shown in the bottom left-hand corner.

Control toolbars

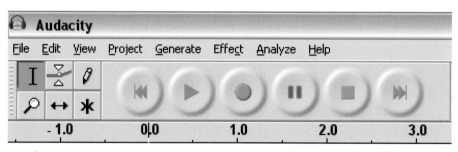

| I | Selection tool – for selecting a section of the track that you want to edit |
| Envelope tool – for changing the audio amplitude (volume) by section |
| Draw tool – for modifying or moving individual samples (use at high zoom) |
| Zoom tool – for zooming in and out, extending or shortening the timeline |
| Timeshift tool – for sliding tracks left or right to synchronise events |
| Multi tool – enables the use of any tool, controlled by the keyboard and mouse position |

Creating a new project and recording sound

To make a new sound recording:

1. Set the audio I/O preferences for the number of channels you will be recording, that is, when recording stereo use a value of '2'.
2. Plug a microphone into the 'Mic' socket.
3. Perform a sound check to make sure that the volume levels are suitable. Adjust the recording volume level as needed (click on the level meter itself to monitor this before starting to record). The sound levels should stay within and use most of the meter window.
4. Make sure that there will be no background distractions during the recording.
5. Click on the red 'Record' button to start.

You can 'Pause' or 'Stop' the recording at any time by clicking on the appropriate button.

Mixer toolbar

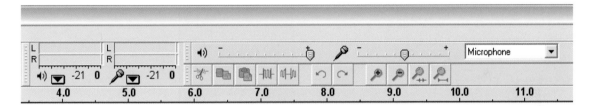

This has four sections from left to right:

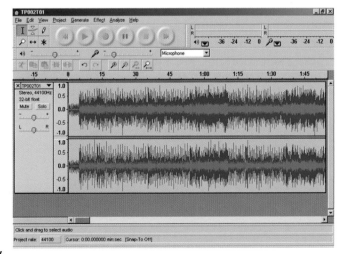

1. Recording and playback level meters (identified by the speaker and microphone symbols)
2. Playback volume slider
3. Recording volume slider
4. Input source selection (shown for microphone)

Note that mono recordings will only have a single audio waveform and volume level, which will be labelled as the 'Left' channel.

Noise removal

Sometimes this is needed to clean up the sound recordings. The procedure in Audacity is:

- Make a selection of a section of the track that is meant to be silent (i.e. it only has background noise).
- Select 'Noise Removal' from the Effects menu and then 'Get Noise Profile' (this stores information about the noise profile, which is used in the next step).
- Make a new selection of the whole track that has the noise that needs to be removed.
- Select 'Noise Removal' from the 'Effects' menu again and click on 'Remove Noise'.

Track control panel

This is displayed alongside each track. It shows the track name and properties, and provides the track drop-down menu. The top slider is the gain control (volume) and the bottom slider is the left/right balance on stereo tracks.

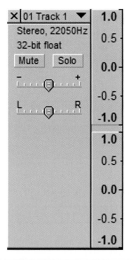

Trim and cut tools

In Audacity, you use the selection tool to click and drag on the section that you want from the track waveform display. In this track, a selection has been made between 10:40 and 14:45 on the timeline.

Once selections have been made, a range of editing effects can be applied.

For any selection, the following tools can be used to trim cut, copy paste, etc:

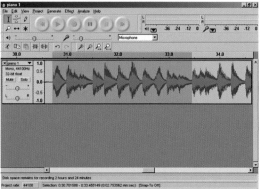

The 'Edit' menu has additional commands to split and duplicate selections into new tracks.

Labels can be placed at various points on the tracks as markers. These can be used to identify specific events and locate special sections but are only saved in Audacity Project Files (.aup).

Audio level compression

This type of compression reduces the dynamic range of the sound so that high volume levels are not quite as high as originally recorded. This helps to maintain a more consistent volume level between normal sound levels and the loudest parts. First, make a selection of the waveform. From the 'Effects' menu choose 'Compressor'. The amount of compression and the point where it is applied can be chosen, although the default values are a good starting point.

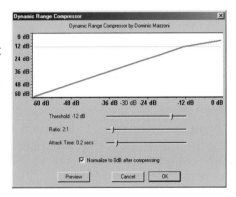

The envelope tool in Audacity is used to modify the amplitude envelope of the audio track. Click on any position in the waveform and drag the envelope up or down. Individual samples can also be moved up/down using the draw tool when zoomed in close enough to identify each data sample point.

Mixing or combining multiple sound tracks

Two separate sound files can be mixed as follows:

1. Open the first file (e.g. background music).
2. Open the second file (e.g. voiceover) using 'import audio'.
3. Play the combined sound to check for timing, clarity, volume and any clipping.
4. Adjust the gain controls for each track to balance the sounds as required.
5. Use the time shift tool to change the timing or synchronisation of the two tracks.
6. Export as a new file in a suitable format.

Adding effects

These can only be applied to current selections. Commonly used basic effects are:

- **Amplify:** changes the volume (amplitude) of the current selection.
- **Fade in:** fades in the current selection from silence to full volume.
- **Fade out:** fades out the current selection from full volume to silence.

Mono/stereo conversion

This can be set from the track drop-down menu on the track control panel:

- **Mono:** plays on a single speaker or duplicates the same signal for use with two speakers.
- **Left:** forces the sound to be on the left channel (speaker) only.
- **Right:** forces the sound to be on the right channel (speaker) only.
- **Make stereo:** when there is a second track below the current one, Audacity can merge the two tracks to create a single stereo track. For stereo tracks, the top track is the left channel and the bottom track is the right channel.

Saving sound files

2 Objective (3c)

From Audacity, you can export the sound into one of several different formats depending on how you want to use the file.

.aup	You can save files in this format but this is an Audacity Project File. It can only be used for further editing and is not a generic format for export or playing on other audio equipment.
.mp3	Requires a LAME encoder to be installed separately for use by the Audacity software (due to mp3 intellectual property licensing restrictions). It is a popular format with good performance and file size compression.
WAV	Windows Wave format without any compression. Files will be larger than mp3 but there is no reduction in sound quality using this format.
Ogg Vorbis	An effective format similar to mp3 but slightly better performance in terms of file size/sound quality. Not well supported for playback on other audio devices.

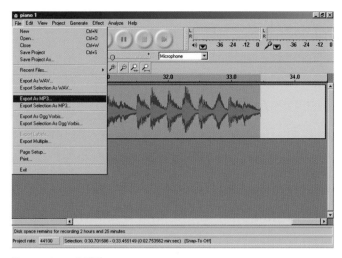

Export as MP3

Comparison of file sizes in different formats:

Track information:	Duration: 1 minute, 16-bit, 44.1 kHz
WAV (uncompressed)	5500kB (5.5MB)
mp3	1000kB (1MB)
Ogg Vorbis	660kB (0.66MB)

After you have exported the sound files, play them back using the target player or equipment. This is necessary to make sure that the file format is correct and the volume level is suitable for the intended use.

Digital sound projects

In your assignment, you will use a computer software program to create your digital sound files. Examples of digital sound projects that you could produce are:

- **Voiceovers:** For this you will need to develop a script, find somebody to read and record them (it does not have to be you). Think about the timing of the script as well as the content, using cues as appropriate.
- **Effects:** These could be Foley effects for specific actions or events (see below).
- **Music:** This can be a musical performance on stage or a single piece played in a studio. Think about whether this will need

microphones or MIDI connections and how you will control the background sounds. Microphone choice will be important.

Creating Foley effects

Definition: A Foley artist is somebody who creates sounds in a studio for specific effects. For example, this may be footsteps on a wooden floor that is needed for a video clip. If the video camera was positioned far enough away so as not to record the actual sound, it would need to be added later. Therefore it must be created in a studio and synchronised with the video clip.

The following table describes how some Foley effects can be created:

Sound effect	How to create it (just think about the timing)
Bird flying	Flap a pair of leather gloves, one in each hand.
Breaking bones	Snap a piece of celery, carrot or lettuce.
Footsteps	Put a pair of shoes on your hands and 'walk' on a table.
Footsteps in snow	Squeeze half a packet of flour or corn starch in a cloth or leather bag (paper makes its own noise).
Galloping horses	Bang coconut shells together.
Kissing	Kiss the back of your hand or arm.
Walking on grass	Scrunch old video or audio tape in your hands.

This next exercise is great fun and will develop your creative talents with digital sound. Don't just skip over this one. . .

PRACTICE EXERCISE

Create your own Foley effects

1. Research more examples of how Foley effects are made.
2. Set up your recording equipment with a suitable microphone and software settings.
3. Use coconut shells, leather gloves, packets of flour or anything else that you need…
4. Complete a sound check and record the sound effects, making sure that the microphone and volume levels are suitable for what you need.
5. Trim, edit, add effects and save the files in an appropriate format.
6. Try combining effects in a sequence to produce a short story! Make sure that you plan the story first to identify what the sounds will be and how they can be created.

Creating ambient and natural sounds

Carefully choose either an omni-directional or cardioid microphone depending on where the actual sound is being produced. For example, if it is a waterfall then a cardioid or super-cardioid microphone pointed at the water would work well. Alternatively, if you are in the middle of the action and want to record sounds from a football field and crowd, then an omni-directional may be better. Check the audio levels and stay quiet during the recording!

Creating music sounds

Here you have the choice of recording using a microphone or possibly by MIDI connection. For example, if you want to record the playing of an electronic keyboard there may well be a MIDI out socket that you can connect directly to your recording equipment. This will record the 'pure' sound without any background or ambient sounds – so you could be talking at the same time and it would not matter. Your computer may have separate volume settings for MIDI recording so check these and test everything before you start.

Using other software

The screen layout varies but the three basic sections in any software are:

1. Recording sound
2. Editing sound using the tools and menus
3. Graphical display area of the digital sound.

The basic processes and concepts of creating digital sound are also the same whatever software is being used. These are:

1. Record or import the sound into a new project.
2. Save the sound tracks.
3. Clean up, trim and cut tracks as required.
4. Import soundtracks, voiceover, music tracks and mix as required.
5. Export the finished sound in a suitable format.

When using different software for the first time, identify how to do the basics and then build your knowledge of the extra features as needed.

There are a number of other software options for digital sound editing. We take a brief look at some of these on the following pages.

Using Adobe Audition

The Audition GUI is made up of several sections:

- At the top of the screen, shortcut icons are found on a toolbar for cutting, trimming, mixing, editing the envelope and changing the track properties.
- The main workspace has a multi-track view and an edit view. The multi-track view is used to combine and mix sounds for the final work. The edit view is used to work on a single track.
- The panel at the left-hand side provides tabs for files, effects and favourites. Use the files tab to manage the digital sound files in your project. Audio effects can be added easily by switching to the effects or favourites tab.
- At the bottom of the window you find the playback and zoom controls, just above the timeline and volume displays.

Using Adobe Soundbooth

This is part of Adobe Creative Suite 3. The Soundbooth GUI has a basic set of panels and user-friendly workspace layout:

- Panels are found at the left-hand side for file management, common tasks, effects and editing history.
- To record a new sound, select 'File' menu > 'Record'. The sound input recording properties and volume levels are checked before starting to record.
- Recorded (or imported) sounds are edited using the Tasks and Effects panels.
- Playback controls and the timeline are found at the bottom of the screen.
- To save the new sound files, choose 'File' menu > 'Save As. . .'

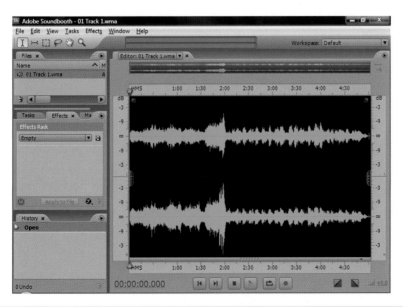

Using Apple Garageband

This is a part of the iLife suite from Apple for use on a Mac computer.

Garageband allows you to create, record and edit digital sound files.

- The workspace has the tracks assembled on a timeline as usual, with track information shown at the left-hand side. Playback controls and information panels are found at the bottom of the screen.
- When selected, the sound file/project information is displayed in a new panel at the right-hand side of the screen.
- New tracks can be created as:
  - Software instrument: using MIDI, USB or on-screen keyboard
  - Real instrument: recording voice, music or other sounds using a microphone.
- Files are saved as .band files and exported in different formats from the 'Share' menu.

PART 4: REVIEWING DIGITAL SOUND PROJECTS

2 Objective (3d)

2 Objective (4a)

When reviewing project work on creating digital sounds, there will be a number of questions to ask:

1. Does the sound meet the needs of the client?
2. Is the sound file size suitable for the client and target audience?

3. Is the sound file format suitable for the client and target audience?
4. Is the quality of the sound suitable in terms of clarity, tone and SNR (signal-to-noise ratio)?
5. Is the sound editing effective?
6. Is the audio mixing suitable (where used)?
7. Does the final work demonstrate a conventional or creative/innovative approach? There is no right or wrong here – just recognise what has been produced.
8. What improvements could be made – for example in equipment, sound recording techniques and/or editing?

You may want to obtain some constructive comments from friends and the client in order to answer these questions. You could also refer to the general comments in the section on Planning and Review in the Introduction.

SUMMARY

In this unit we have covered digital sound technology, its uses, applications, recording and creation. It is by developing skills with the use of microphones and recording equipment, in addition to the software, that will enable you to create a wide range of digital sound projects. Perhaps you will also have experimented with Foley effects during the recording and editing of your sounds. Remember that sound editing techniques can be changed if something doesn't work but sometimes it can be difficult to go back and re-record a sound. Good quality sound recording will be the best foundation for producing high-quality digital sound content.

FINAL ASSIGNMENT

Once you have learned all the required parts of the unit, you will complete an assignment that will be used to assess your knowledge and skills of the subject. It will be set in a vocational context, which means that it will simulate what it would be like to be given a project by a client or employer in a work situation. To start you should read the brief or scenario carefully to identify what is needed. A typical assignment may be in the following format (although these should not be used as templates for designing your own assignments – refer to the guidance documents on the OCR website for this purpose):

> *Brief:*
>
> *You are a junior sound technician for Tulipa Rossa sports goods and have been asked to produce some new sounds that can be used on their new website. For this you will need to record a range of sounds on a sporting theme and combine them to create a 30-second sound clip.*
>
> *Task 1: Here you may be asked to explore a range of appropriate sound recording hardware and software along with the suitable file formats for the final work.*
>
> *Task 2: In this task you will be asked to plan the development of your work. Use one or more of the planning methods described in the Introduction, identifying what you will need and how long it is likely to take.*
>
> *Task 3: In this task you will be asked to actually produce or create your work. This should demonstrate a range of skills using sound recording technology and sound editing software. You will also need to test the finished sound files to make sure the file size/format is suitable for the client brief.*
>
> *Task 4: In this task you should review your final work. This means thinking about things like overall quality, fitness for purpose and any areas for improvement. It is not just a summary of how you created the work – it should be a reflection by yourself (and others) on how suitable it is for use by the client described in the brief.*

Note that essential parts of the assignment include the planning and reviewing of your work. It is important to be able to think about what you need to produce and what the final work should look like. Since the assignment is in a vocational context it will be important to check the suitability of what you have produced before submitting it to the client. The development of these skills will be a great benefit when you are asked to produce something in the real/commercial world of employment.

Digital Video

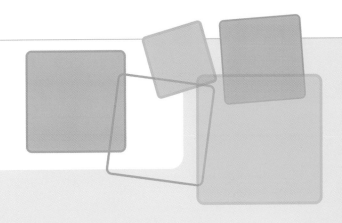

The aim of this unit is to develop knowledge, skills and understanding in the use of digital video cameras and video editing software applications. You will learn how to use a digital video camera to record footage, transfer it to a computer and edit the clips to produce the final cut of a short video.

Note: This chapter covers all of the knowledge and skills required for:

1 Unit 5

2 Unit 6

- Level 1 Unit 5 (Digital sound and video)
- Level 2 Unit 6 (Digital video)

PART 1: TECHNOLOGY USED TO PRODUCE DIGITAL VIDEO

2 Objective (1a)

2 Objective (1b)

Explore video technology

DV is a general term for any form of digital video. Before DV was developed, video recording was based on analogue film, which required specialist skills and equipment to edit. With digital video, the light detected by the camera sensor is sampled very quickly to produce digital data that is stored on tape, DVD or hard disk.

MiniDV is a high-performance digital video tape format. It stores the information in a digital format (not analogue like a piece of film) and can be transferred to a computer for non-linear editing,

which means that clips can be easily moved around on a timeline. Advances in technology have made it much cheaper to be able to record and edit video. Entry-level camcorders can be good value for money and many other devices can now record video as well (such as compact cameras and mobile phones).

The video industry used to have specific job functions, such as a cameraman and video editor. These roles have merged in smaller video productions so that one person will need a range of skills in recording sound and video footage with the camera as well as editing the work to produce a final cut. Hence you will develop skills in a wide range of areas for this unit. In the same way as digital graphics, good editing cannot create miracles if the original sound and video are poor quality. For instance, camera shake cannot be taken out by editing, so it is best to use a tripod when recording the original footage.

Where, when and why do we use digital video?

Some examples of the use of video are:

- film
- television
- World Wide Web
- portable entertainment
- multimedia
- music videos
- commercial advertising and promotion (for use on CDs and/or websites).

Digital video is also popular with home users to record holidays, weddings and other family events.

The skills involved in basic video editing for this unit may also be used to convert older video formats for use on the Web or to create movies that can play back on a home DVD player. This process begins with capturing the original footage to the computer.

If saving video for use on the Web, high quality is not yet needed because the available bandwidth is relatively low. As the speed of Internet connections increases, the quality of video needed for Web use will increase. When choosing video equipment for recording footage don't just think about what quality we need for the Web today. Within a few years Web videos will support higher resolutions and quality.

Ask friends and family whether they have a video camera. You might even have one on your mobile phone. This is a good way to introduce the basic concepts – record some footage and find out how to copy it to your computer.

Genre

In video terms, this is the type or category of the script or storyline. Examples would be:

- action/adventure
- comedy
- drama
- documentary
- horror
- romantic
- thriller.

The choice of genre will be influenced by the needs of the client, the creative style of the video producer and the target audience. For example, a promotional video for a business is likely to be in a documentary style, whereas horror is most likely to be inappropriate. On the other hand, a music video for a pop song could be interpreted as drama, action/adventure, romantic or even light comedy. The video producer may have more creative control of the way this video is made, although ideas would still have to be approved by the end client.

Note that a film or movie genre is different to a game genre and the categories do differ. The visual style, lighting and types of shots used will be dependant on the chosen genre.

Audiences

As well as responding to the needs of the client, the video producer also needs to know who the target audience is for the final video. Think about who the audience is and what their interests and needs are. Things to consider are:

- age group
- gender (male/female)
- interests.

Video standards, resolutions and aspect ratios

Video resolution is defined by the number of pixels in each frame. The aspect ratio is the ratio of width to height of the frame, so a 4:3 aspect ratio could be 40cm wide and 30cm high (the actual sizes will vary but the ratio will stay the same).

Analogue broadcast television standards

Parameter	PAL	NTSC	SECAM
Mains freq	50Hz	60Hz	50Hz
Frame rate	25fps (50 interlaced fields)	30fps	25fps
Image size (pixels)	720 × 576	720 × 480	720 × 576
Number of lines	625	525	625
Aspect ratio	4:3	4:3	4:3
Regions/countries	UK, Europe, Far East, Australia	US, parts of South America	France, Russia, Africa, Eastern Europe

Digital television standards

Analogue broadcast television is being phased out in the UK, to be replaced by digital television. This means that the broadcast of TV channels is in a digital rather than analogue (wave) format. Freeview channels are examples of digital broadcasting.

High-definition digital television is a relatively new digital video standard that provides higher resolution for use on larger display screens. The aspect ratio is also different for use with widescreen displays.

Parameter	HD 720p	HD 1080i
Frame rate	25fps	25fps
Image size (pixels)	1080 × 720	1440 × 1080
Number of lines	720 progressive	1080 interlaced
Aspect Ratio	16:9	16:9

Audio settings

- **Mono:** This is a single-sound channel suitable for use with one speaker.
- **Stereo:** This is a two-channel sound system with left and right channels, requiring two or more speakers.
- **Surround sound:** This is a multi-channel sound system with speakers in front of and behind the listener. HD TV has Dolby 5.1 surround sound built in to drive five speakers. More recently, 7.1 surround sound has been developed, which uses seven speakers.

Digital video cameras have built-in microphones for recording sound with the video footage. This is captured to the computer at the same time as the video and can be edited or replaced with a different soundtrack. The use of a suitable external microphone will usually give better results.

Camera fitted with external microphone

Compression formats and codecs

The process of video compression discards some information in order to make the file size smaller. The overall quality of the digital video will depend on how much compression and what codec is used. The codec is the compression–decompression process (or encoder–decoder). Examples of codecs include MPEG-1, MPEG-2, MPEG-4, DivX and Windows Media Video (WMV). Another example is H.264, which is high-performance MPEG-4 (AVC) or Advanced Video Coding. In particular, this is a video compression standard that enables high-quality video over low-bandwidth (384kbps) Internet connections.

Compared to MiniDV format, the codec that creates MPEG files will discard information from frames where something does not move, for example a static background when using a tripod. If a scene has no movement it may only store one complete frame for each second of footage even though the playback frame rate could still be 25fps (frames per second).

Some newer video cameras are available that store recorded footage directly in a high-definition AVCHD format. If using this type of camera, check your video editing software can handle this format before recording the footage.

Equipment for recording and working with video

Computer hardware to capture and edit video

Both PC and Apple Mac computers are used for video editing applications. Creative graphics sound and video represent typical uses for Apple Macs, and Macs have maintained their popularity in these fields. Most software applications are called 'non-linear editors' (NLE). This means that video clips can be edited and moved around on a timeline in the computer software. Non-linear editing and digital video capture in general produce a large amount of data and files can be very large. Serious use will need specialised computers, with dual processors, extra-large secondary disks, twin monitors, and a large amount of RAM. You will need writable CD/DVD/Blu-Ray drives to burn a disc with your final cut. You will also need high-performance sound and video cards for anything other than basic video.

A standard PC or Mac can still be used, but keep the working files within reasonable limits. Many MiniDV video cameras use a FireWire connection, which is a high-speed serial connection to transfer video. Not many cameras use USB unless they are hard-disk recorders or work as a webcam.

Computer requirements

	PC	Mac
CPU (Processor)	Modern processor such as Pentium® 4, Pentium® M or Celeron®	G4 or G5
Memory	The more the better; at least 512MB is required but 1GB or more is a practical size.	The more the better; 512MB to 1GB is practical for most applications.
Hard disk (internal or external)	Video capture and editing can create very large files, so a second dedicated disk is a good option.	
CD/DVD or Blu-Ray/HD-DVD	CD writer is needed to create VCD (video CD). DVD rewriter is required to create playable DVD movies.	
Video card(s)	A minimum 16-bit colour graphics card is required.	
Sound card	This is essential for monitoring sound quality and dubbing (adding new sound tracks).	
FireWire	Interface port for connection to MiniDV cameras. Laptops often have one built in but desktop computers may require an expansion card to be fitted.	There is a standard port on Apple computers so no additional cards are required.
USB	This is a standard communication port, which is used to connect to DVD or hard-disk video cameras. USB cannot be used with MiniDV cameras to capture footage.	
Display	At least 1024 × 768 pixels. Pro-video editors may use two monitors on a single computer.	

Video equipment (cameras and accessories)

In this section we will look at the equipment you will need to record the original footage. This includes digital video cameras and a range of accessories that can be used to improve the recording.

Types of digital video camera

The different types can be grouped by their recording format or medium:

- **MiniDV:** This was originally a format produced by Sony but it is now supported by a wide range of manufacturers. It is still very popular and has still has some advantages over HD (high definition) format.
- **DVCAM:** DVCAM is a slightly larger cassette tape format when compared to MiniDV, which also runs at a higher tape speed. It is often found on Sony professional or semi-pro cameras as they originally developed the format.
- **MicroMV:** This is a physically smaller tape size than MiniDV that has the same resolution. However, the data rate is only half that of MiniDV and it also uses MPEG-2 compression. As mentioned earlier, this is not quite so good if you will be using more advanced editing techniques.
- **Digital8:** This is also a digital format found on some older cameras. It records the same information and data as MiniDV except that it uses a Hi8 tape.
- **DVD (or DVD-Video using DVD-R or DVD-RAM):** For those who do not want to capture and edit footage on a computer, the convenience of being able to play DVD discs directly from the camera on a home player can be attractive. The video data files can still be edited using video editing software although the video is stored in an MPEG-2 format that has significant compression already applied.
- **HDD (Hard Disk Devices):** This is not related to high definition but instead refers to the use of mechanical hard disks to store the video footage. These hard disks are the same as found in computers and the video is stored in a format that can be copied directly from the camera disk to the computer disk. The video files again use MPEG-2 compression and can store many hours of footage.
- **HDV:** This has proved popular despite using MPEG-2 compression. It has a significantly higher resolution so the playback on high definition television is much sharper. There are two main sizes, developed by JVC and Sony. Note that standard definition PAL video uses a resolution of 720 × 576 pixels.

- **HD-720p:** This was developed by JVC and uses a resolution of 1280 × 720 pixels. Effectively, this has twice the pixel resolution of standard PAL video.
- **HD-1080i:** This was developed by Sony and uses 1440 × 1080 pixels. Effectively, this is four times the pixel resolution of standard PAL. This produces sharp pictures on larger HD televisions of 40 inches or more.

Older analogue video camera formats include:

- **VHS-C:** This uses the same format as VHS tapes but in a more compact tape size. Adapters enable the tapes to be played on standard VHS players.
- **S-VHS:** This is Super VHS, which is a higher quality than standard VHS.
- **Hi8:** This is similar to S-VHS in that it is higher quality than standard VHS.

Mobile phones and digital compact cameras currently have a very low resolution, low frame rate and use high compression before saving video files. The footage could be used for low-resolution web videos, although the capabilities will improve rapidly over the next few years.

- **Consumer video camera types:** These tend to be smaller, easier to carry around and in a range of prices and video quality. When choosing a camera the main features to look at are the recording format, size/resolution of the sensor and the optical zoom range.
- **Semi-pro video cameras:** These are physically larger than consumer-style camcorders. They have more manual controls, a higher-quality build and recording quality.

Key components and specifications of digital video cameras

Charge Coupled Device (CCD)	This is the light-sensing component in the camera. A large number of entry-level cameras will have 800,000 pixels although standard PAL definition is only 414,720 (720 × 576). Cameras that have a larger number of pixels can use the information for 'in camera' image stabilization. The physical size of the CCD will affect the light sensitivity. Typical values are 1/6' or 1/4' and larger sensors usually allow the camera to be used more effectively in low light. Cameras with three CCDs have one CCD per colour (red/green/blue). These produce higher-quality video with good colour reproduction, especially in low light.
Lens	Video cameras are fitted with zoom lenses that allow you to magnify the image in the viewfinder. The only important type is optical zoom, which is a true optical magnification. Digital zoom reduces image quality and is better left alone unless the footage is only going to be used for the Web at low resolution.
LCD	This is usually a 'flip out' screen that can be used for monitoring the recording. It also provides access to the menu functions and camera setup.
Viewfinder	When shooting outdoors in bright daylight, this is often better than the built-in LCD, which can be difficult to see properly. Using the viewfinder instead of the LCD will also increase the battery time.
Microphone	Video cameras have a built-in microphone although recordings can pick up sound from all directions – even your own mutterings and the motor for the zoom lens. Much better results can be obtained by using an external microphone. (Refer to Chapter 6 Digital Sound for more information).
Image stabilization	In-camera stabilization is a poor substitute for a good tripod. Hand-holding the camera usually adds a lot of movement or camera 'wobble'. If choosing a camera, optical image stabilization will be more effective than digital but this largely depends on whether you will be using a tripod in most of your recording.
Menu	This gives access to camera settings such as 'auto' and 'manual' controls, white balance, focusing, sound format, date/time, display information and timecode.

Camera connections

Socket	Description	Identification
FireWire, i.Link or IEEE1394	This is found on MiniDV cameras. It is a high-speed communication port for transferring video from the camera to computer. Some cameras also have an i.Link 'IN' connection to store edited video back onto the MiniDV tape.	
USB	Hard-disk cameras will have this type of connection instead of FireWire. Some MiniDV cameras may have both FireWire and USB although the USB port is used to transfer still images and webcam video streams for low-resolution use on a computer.	
S-Video	This is a 'Separate Video' signal with two wires for luminance (brightness) and chrominance (colour) in one cable.	
Audio/Video	There are three separate RCA connectors for composite video (yellow) and audio (white = left or mono, red = right)	
Microphone	Most cameras have a socket for an external microphone. On consumer models this will usually be a 3.5mm socket but semi-pro cameras will have XLR-style connectors. This larger type of connector can also provide 'phantom' power to high-performance condenser microphones (refer to Chapter 6 Digital Sound for more information on microphones).	
DC Power	This is an external power supply connection which also recharges the battery.	

Video camera accessories

Batteries

Video cameras use a lot of power and the standard battery supplied with a camera will not power it for very long – perhaps less than one hour. It is a good idea to carry spares and higher-capacity versions are available for extended shooting on location or when away from mains power.

Tripods

Tripods are almost essential if you are to produce professional-quality results. Video cameras cannot be held steady by hand and watching video footage that is jumping around is quite difficult. Try recording a short clip – one on a tripod and one hand-held. Use a pan/tilt technique and a zoom. Look at both clips on a large-screen monitor (TV or computer screen) to compare the results. A 'tripod' has two main parts – the tripod legs and the head. Popular choices for video use are 'fluid heads' that give very smooth panning and vertical movement.

External microphones

These generally produce better sound recordings than the microphones that are built into video cameras. The choice of microphone is important to make sure the sensitivity and directionality is suitable for what you want to record. Examples include directional (shotgun) and tie-clip (lavalier) microphones. These are described in more detail in Chapter 6 Digital Sound. If the camera has a headphone socket, use it to monitor the sound quality when recording the original footage.

Lights

You will need to control the lighting to give the best video footage. Sometimes this means providing the lights for the subject. These lights will need their own power, either mains or battery. Note that when using accessory lights, you will need to set the white balance (WB) correctly on the camera in order to capture the colours accurately. Camera-mounted lights give the same direct lighting effect as a flashgun mounted on a digital stills camera. If possible, position the light off to one side for a more pleasant effect with natural shadows.

Filters

Filters can be fitted to the front of the lens for special effects and corrections. Examples are:

- Neutral density (used to reduce the depth of field some semi-pro cameras have this built in)
- Polarizing (increases the contrast and reduces reflections from water and other surfaces)
- Colour correction (e.g. when using accessory lights)
- Special visual effects (star burst or diffusion spots)

Video cases

Cases are meant to protect the equipment rather than just look nice. Use something with good padding that is also waterproof, especially if you are working outside a lot.

Sticky tape (e.g. electricians' or masking)

Sticky tape fixes and holds many different things in position such as accessories, props, subject or background. It can also help to prevent people tripping over loose cables that are laid across the floor.

PART 2: PLANNING DIGITAL VIDEO PROJECTS

1 Objective (2)

2 Objective (2b)

Before pre-production you will still need to know what is required for the video project. This will be described in a client brief or specification. Read this document carefully and think about how to satisfy the needs of the client using your own creative talents and ideas. Note down some ideas on how to complete the video shoot or you could make some sketches of the visual style. Also think about what genre the video could fit into. If it is for a sports product would you take a conventional documentary style approach, action/adventure or perhaps comedy? Discuss all of your ideas with the client before starting work on the pre-production and recording of footage. Don't forget to ask about whether any key items need to be included in the video footage, such as a pair of training shoes if it is going to be for a sports product.

Of course you will need to document any use of copyrighted, trademarked or intellectual property. Keep records of all sources and permissions obtained for any material that is not your own using the form provided on the CD (or an equivalent).

Finally, think about how long the whole project will take. After your initial discussions with the client, they will want to know this; break the time down into timescales for pre-production, recording of footage and video editing.

Plan pre-production

2 Objective (2b)

Before recording any video footage, it is important to plan what you are going to do. Good results come from good planning, so let's start with a *storyboard*.

Creating a storyboard

This is a series of sketches or diagrams of what each type of scene/shot will be and how it will be created. Additional information can be included to identify camera angles, movement and lighting. A key part of a storyboard is that it illustrates the *story that is being told* and has a timeline associated with it. On the next page is an example of a storyboard for a video shoot. A template for a storyboard can also be found on the CD supplied with this book, in both Microsoft Word® and Adobe PDF formats.

Note: A 'shot' is a single uninterrupted series of frames or film footage. A storyboard will comprise a number of different scenes, frames and/or shots.

Preparing a script and characters

In addition to the storyboard, the preparation of a script may be necessary if you have people talking or being interviewed in the video. If producing a short film, the actors will need to know what to say and when. This is what the script is for. A basic example would be:

Pre-Production Storyboard

Title and intro (Text and name)	
Short intro clip, 5 seconds max	Opening scene
Create in video editing software	Long shot, showing landscape
	Pan camera left to right (on tripod)

	Tag line
Single person, being interviewed	Closing scene, 5 seconds
Medium shot	Fade in closing credits
(Script to be prepared)	

Scene location: John and Alice are talking to each other using a mobile phone.	
John	{Ring} {Ring} [Answers phone call] *Hello!*
Alice	[Smiles] *Hi John, have you tried your new high-definition television yet?*
John	[Smiles] *Hi Alice. Yes – I used it with my games console last night.*
Alice	[Curious] *I was wondering what it was like to watch a movie.*
John	[Smiles a bit more] *Why don't you come over and see for yourself?*
Alice	[Ecstatic] *I will – see you soon, bye!*

A script can also be marked up to identify what type of camera shot will be used. This information is given to the camera operator to set up the recording as required by the director.

Choosing and preparing equipment for the shoot

With a client brief, storyboard and script you probably have enough information to choose what equipment you will need for the video shoot. In addition to the video camera and any accessories, you will also need recording tapes or DVD (unless using a hard-disk recorder). MiniDV tapes can be 'striped' first to lay down the timecode onto the tape. This means inserting a new tape and putting the camera on 'record' with the lens cap on for the duration of the tape. You only need to do this once and is not essential, but if you are likely to record and playback sections it is a safer way to use tapes. The reason is that non-linear editing software needs to see a continuous timecode through the whole tape. Otherwise it may not capture the correct footage from the right place. The timecode is a standard format for identifying the unique position or frame in a tape. It is in the format of: hours:minutes:seconds:frames. If there is a break in the timecode, it could restart at 00:00:00:00 part way through the tape and conflict with the correct 00:00:00:00, which is at the beginning.

When using hard-disk and DVD types of camera, remember that compression techniques will be used when saving the video in MPEG-2 format. This means that some information will be lost, especially in the parts of the frame that are not moving (usually the background). This type of video footage will not be as good for editing purposes. Trim and cuts, transitions and blending is fine but if you want to make significant changes to the content of the footage, bear in mind that a tape format such as MiniDV will have recorded high-quality footage in all parts of the frame. Because we are looking at basic editing techniques at Level 1 and 2, this is not a big concern. If there is a possibility of wanting to do more advanced editing at a later time, think about what type of video camera and recording format will be most suitable.

Selecting location

Depending on what video footage is being recorded, you may be able to choose your own suitable location and background. Try to find somewhere that will not have distractions going on behind the main subject or people. Use either a static or plain background or consider using a shallow depth of field to put the background out of focus (but keeping the subject sharp). The depth of field is controlled by the iris (aperture) size, that is, a larger iris = less depth of field.

Unless you are going to add the sound in later at the editing stage, you probably want to record a good-quality soundtrack at the same time as the video footage. As mentioned previously, careful choice of microphone and the directionality will minimise the effects of background noise. If you have a directional (shotgun) microphone, make sure that it is pointed at the mouth of the person who is speaking for the best audio quality. If using the built-in microphones on video cameras, they will record sound from any direction. Even the motor for the zoom lens can be picked up on some cameras as well as traffic noise or people talking in the background. Try a test-shoot first and use a set of headphones to listen to the sound recording quality.

Production design

Unless shooting a documentary or event, you may have the ability to control the scene as well. This is another part of the planning process where you can decide what the set will look like and even what people should wear. 'Set dressing' is the term used to describe the steps you take to create the scene for the video recording. 'Props' are items that you can use in the scene to enhance or support the main subject.

Creative considerations

Composition in the viewfinder can use the same rules of photography as for still images (see Chapter 2 Digital Graphics for more information). You might want to position people or other key subjects using the rule of thirds for example. Aim to record your footage as the final composition. Unlike still images, it is not easy to crop the frames in the editing while maintaining good image quality. Compositional considerations would be:

- using the rule of thirds
- using lines and perspective to emphasise shape and depth
- using frames (above, below and to the sides)
- foreground interest in wide-angle landscape shots
- leaving more space in front of a moving object, not behind.

In addition to the main footage, plan to record additional footage that could be used to enhance the final video clip. This could include more general scenes and panoramas that could be used as cutaways (which are short pieces of footage used in between scenes or shots to provide additional information).

The visual style of the video will depend on what the final use is going to be and is decided at the planning stage. For instance, if you are recording a video blog or somebody reading a news story, they will most likely be looking straight into camera. On the other hand, movies are nearly always shot in the third-person view, that is, none of the characters look into the camera and the person watching the video is just an invisible observer.

PART 3: RECORD, CAPTURE, EDIT AND SAVE DIGITAL VIDEO

| 1 | Objective (2) |
| 2 | Objective (3a) |

Using a digital video camera to record footage

Enough theory – you will learn a lot by picking up a video camera and actually using it. Make sure that the battery is fully charged or use the mains adapter to power the camera. If practical, set the camera up on a tripod and go through your checks on lighting, camera settings and movement.

Ambient lighting

Basic questions to ask are:

1. Is there enough light?
2. What type of light is it?
3. Where is it coming from?

If the light level is very low, the footage will not be very high quality. There may be some colour noise and blurred movement (due to a slow shutter speed being used by the camera). Ambient light can be natural (daylight) or artificial (indoor light bulbs), which affects what camera settings are needed to make sure that the colours record accurately (see the next section). The direction and strength of the lighting will also affect shadows on any people and subjects. If a single light source is used, look carefully at where the shadows fall and see if additional lights could be used to improve the ambience or mood of the shot. Finally, think about the genre for the video – this can provide ideas about what lighting effects to use. For example, horror could be quite dark with a single light source and documentary could be bright and well balanced.

Camera settings

After switching the camera on there are two basic modes – recording and playback. If you want to record new footage, make sure that you are using the recording mode. Try to get familiar with the following basic camera settings and controls:

- how to start and stop the recording
- how to use the lens zoom control
- changing from recording to playback mode
- rewinding the tape and playing back the recorded video on the LCD.

Practise these steps so you can do them comfortably as it can be difficult if somebody is waiting for you to get the camera running. If using a camera for the first time, leave it on 'Auto' and just think about the framing, zoom and holding it steady.

After you have some experience in using the camera on Auto, you can fine-tune some of the settings for better results.

Lens focus

In recording mode, the auto-focus will constantly adjust the focus point to whatever subject is in the middle of the frame. If you are using some camera movement, such as pan and tilt, the focus may move off the subject onto the background and then back again. You may not notice this until the video has been captured to the computer. If you know you want to keep focus at a particular distance, you can change into manual focus mode. Before starting to record, set the focus to where you want it. The best way is to zoom in, focus, zoom out and then start recording.

White balance settings

As mentioned in the section on lighting, the type of light can be natural (daylight) or artificial (e.g. indoor light bulbs and tubes). For the colours to record accurately, the camera has a control function called white balance (WB). If this is set incorrectly, a white object will show up as having either a yellow, green or blue colour cast. This colour

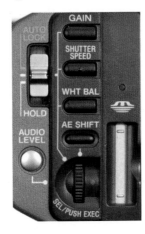

effect is caused by the sensitivity of the camera sensor to the type of lighting. In auto mode, this will be automatically set to what the camera chooses to be the right value. If you know what value is needed for the correct white balance, you can set the camera into manual mode and choose from one of several pre-defined settings. Alternatively, you can custom-tune the white balance using a grey card or semi-transparent lens cover. This is the best way to make sure that colours are recorded accurately for any particular lighting. Refer to your camera instruction manual on how to do this because the methods are different from one camera to another.

Image stabilization

If you do not have a tripod and have to hold the camera by hand, the use of image stabilization will reduce the amount of shake or wobble. Using high-zoom magnification will increase the amount of shake, which can be noticeable even when mounted on a tripod. In these cicumstances, leave the image stabilization turned on.

Camera movement and techniques

There are three basic types of shots:

Long shot

This is taken at distance, such as a panoramic landscape. If a main subject such as a person is in the shot, they will be shown full-length with head and feet. This type of shot is commonly used as an introduction.

Medium shot

A medium shot is taken at mid-distance, with just the upper body shown for people.

Close up shot

This is a detail shot of the action such as a pair of hands or just the face of a person. This type of shot

can also be used as an introduction, followed by zooming out to give the broader picture.

Record a combination of these so that you have more options for creative expression when editing your video clip. The genre and mood will also play a part in the choice of shots taken and used. Once you have some experience of recording these basic shots, you will be able to plan and storyboard new projects using more creative approaches.

Camera movement

Pan and tilt

To pan the camera is to move it from side to side while recording. This technique can be used to show a panoramic landscape or pan between two main subjects. Tilt refers to moving the camera up and down. The use of a fluid head on a tripod will keep these movements smooth.

Zoom

During recording, the camera can be zoomed either in or out. This can also be combined with a pan and tilt to keep the subject where you want it in the frame. Controlling the speed of the zoom can take a bit of practise and be careful of creating too much 'wobble' if hand-holding the camera.

Tracking and dollying

This is a technique of moving the position of the camera while recording. Some tripods can be fitted with wheels so that they can be pushed around on a smooth floor. Alternatively a camera may be mounted on a special platform (a dolly) and moved on a track that is laid out in the direction needed. If hand-holding a camera and walking with it, use your knees to try to keep the height of the camera steady. Just waving the camera around is unlikely to produce pleasing results.

Editing your footage

Video editing software on a computer is referred to as a non-linear editor (NLE). This means that you can select any frame (or series of frames) in the video and move, cut, copy, and so on. You certainly don't have to start at the beginning and work your way through the footage one frame at a time. Drag-and-drop functionality in the software has made editing easier for the occasional user as well as for experienced professionals.

Software options for video editing

Computer type	Software examples
PC	Adobe Premiere Elements®, Adobe Premiere Pro®, Pinnacle Studio®, ULead®, Roxio®, Microsoft Windows® Movie Maker
Apple Mac	iMovie®, Final Cut Pro®, Avid®

Methods of capturing/copying footage

Camera type	Method of capture or connection
MiniDV	FireWire (i.Link) connection – video captured directly into video editing application
DVD camcorder	Finalise the DVD in the camcorder first (this enables the computer to locate the video files on the disc). Insert the DVD into a DVD drive on the main computer and copy the files as required.
HDD (hard disk drive) camcorder	USB connection to transfer video files
HD (high definition) camera	USB connection to transfer video files
Mobile phone or compact camera	USB connection to transfer files or use a card reader with the memory card
Analogue formats (S-VHS, Hi8)	specialised video capture card (internal or external)

Connecting hardware

In addition to the camera and
computer, you will also need a
suitable connection cable for the
communication ports, for example
FireWire (i.Link) or USB.

Capturing footage from
MiniDV tape

Open your video editing software application. In the following
pages we will be using Adobe Premiere Elements 4. You can find an
introduction to alternative software applications later in this chapter.
The initial steps are:

* Arrange the workspace for video capture (click on the capture
  video icon).
* Give the project a name (this will also be used as part of the
  filename for each video clip captured).
* Connect the video camera and make sure that it is in the playback
  mode.
* Capture the video to computer using the playback controls
  provided in the video editing software. If you have used a video
  shot list or edit decision log, it can be used to identify the
  timecode where the required footage is stored.

Click on the 'Get Video' button to capture the footage. If a
particular clip is not required, you can fast forward the tape using
the controls in the video editor capture screen. Footage from a DV
tape will create files of approximately 3.6MB per second (216MB per
minute) so a full 60-minute tape
would need 13GB of disk
space.

Once the capture is complete,
close the capture window and
save the project. Each section of
recorded footage will be
imported onto the Sceneline as a
separate clip. So, if you recorded
10 seconds of footage and then
another 20 seconds, these would
be imported as two clips of 10
seconds and 20 seconds
respectively.

Video projects can be produced either from capturing footage from a camera or by creating a new project and importing media from clips already stored on the computer.

Before we start looking at the editing techniques involved in creating the final cut of a video, let's look at how to create a new project with video clips and other media that are already stored on the computer hard disk in files and folders.

Creating a new project

From the main screen in the video editing software, click on 'New Project'.

You will be prompted for the project name and the location where it will be stored.

The default Project Settings can be changed for the type of video project you are creating. This affects the video format, resolution and sound quality. A range of presets are built in as shown below.

The presets cover video format, resolution, aspect ratio, frame rates and audio settings. Remember that high-quality video and audio can create very large files and you need to consider what the final use will be for the video.

Importing media into the new project

Once you have defined your new project, you will be presented with a blank workspace window.
This is the workspace layout in Adobe Premiere Elements 4.

- The 'Monitor' panel (top left) is used to preview the video clips.
- The 'Tasks' panel (top right) is used to organise, edit and capture media.

- 'My Project' panel is shown at the bottom with the Sceneline/Timeline.

If using the video editing software for the first time, you may want to configure the user preferences from the 'Edit' menu > 'Preferences'. This allows you to change the audio, capture and scratch a disk setting (which is a section on a hard disk used for temporary working files).

To import media for the new project:

- In the 'Tasks' panel, click on the 'Edit' tab to set the workspace for video editing.
- Click on the 'Media' button and then 'Get Media'. This will open a window to browse your computer and locate the files and folders to import the required movie clips (or audio files).
- The imported media files will be shown in the 'Organizer'. Drag and drop these onto the Sceneline and into the sequence that you want to use them. The position of each clip can be changed at any time by dragging and dropping it in the Sceneline.
- To add a background soundtrack, display the timeline view instead of the Sceneline. Drag and drop the audio clip onto the soundtrack from the 'Tasks' panel > 'Edit' tab > 'Media' > 'Organizer'.

Note: If using professional-level video editing software applications such Adobe Premiere CS3®, you will have options to customise the workspace using the panels most appropriate to your work. A brief look at the screen layout for this program is covered at the end of this chapter.

After you have imported your media, the display screen will look something like this (shown using the Sceneline view in the 'My Project' panel).

In the Organizer view of the Task panel, you will see the properties for each asset in the video project. As well as being able to drag and drop, you can also set properties for any asset by right-clicking on it.

Editing the video

1 Objective (3)

2 Objective (3b)

The processes involved in editing video will be similar for whatever software you are using. In the following few pages we will be using Adobe Premiere Elements 4. The skills and techniques will be transferable to most other software and different versions. If you have a clear plan of what you want to achieve, you should be able to apply your knowledge and skills in any video editing software that you have available (remember that there is always a 'Help' menu to support you with adapting to different software applications).

Premiere Elements 4: Main tools and techniques

The Sceneline shows the sequence of video clips, with a preview of the first frame for each clip.

The alternative display at the bottom of the screen is the Timeline. This is a visual representation of the *sequence* of video and audio clips that make up the whole video project.

Tracks

These consist of audio and video clips that are mixed alongside each other. The following diagram shows four basic tracks in the Timeline view:

- Video 1
- Audio 1 (usually recorded with the video)
- Narration (a voiceover that is added to describe the scenes)
- Soundtrack (e.g. background music)

Markers

These are created on the Timeline. They allow a video to be divided into separate video clips that can be selected from a menu when exported to DVD.

Trimming and cutting

In the bottom right-hand corner of the Monitor panel, the scissor icon is used to split a clip at the current point. If you have a clip that you want to trim, click on this icon to split the clip into two parts. You can then select the unwanted clip in the Sceneline and press the delete key to remove it. In addition to cutting, just underneath the split clip is

the time stretch tool. This allows you to speed up or slow down the footage by stretching it over the Timeline.

Audio editing

This involves positioning the audio tracks on the Timeline and adjusting the volume and mixing levels. See 'Adding a soundtrack' later in this chapter.

Rolling edits

This is an editing process that overlays new clips or media with existing clips. This does not extend the total duration.

Split edits

Split edits are where the audio and video start at slightly different times. The video and audio clips can also be dragged or extended along the Timeline. This changes the elapsed duration so that the video appears in slow motion.

Transitions

This is the way the individual clips change from one to another. The default will be a simple changeover, which can be changed to one of many different effects. To change this, right-click on the transition symbol in the Sceneline. A good basic transition is on the dissolve menu – cross dissolve. The transitions used must be appropriate for the visual style and genre chosen.

Title credits

Title credit text can be added using the 'Add default text' tool. Click inside the frame where you want the text to be shown. Once entered, you can change the font and fade effect on the right-hand side of the display.

To preview the video with title credits and additional track layers, you may need to render the video first. If this is needed, a red line will be shown in the timeline. Press the 'Enter' key on the keyboard or select 'Tools' > 'Render the work area'.

Adding a soundtrack

Use the 'Get Media' window to import the required audio track. Drag this onto the Soundtrack in the Timeline.

Use the 'Audio Mixer' window to adjust the relative volume levels of audio, voiceover and soundtracks.

Export/share the video clip

Click on 'Share' in the Tasks panel. To save the video in a format for use on a PC, choose 'Windows Media' from the list. Enter a name for the exported video and check the settings shown at the bottom of the Tasks panel. If you need to optimize the settings to reduce the file size, click on the 'Advanced' button. This allows you to change the audio and video codecs, video frame rate and audio bit depth if required.

The export formats commonly used are:

- DV AVI (PAL standard or widescreen)
- MPEG (PAL VCD, DVD, HD 1080i, H.264 or MPEG-1/MPEG-2)

- Windows Media (.wmv format)
- QuickTime (for Apple computers and Web use)

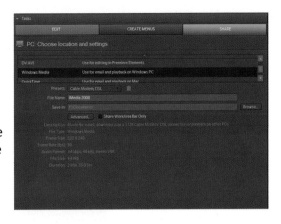

Many of these still have options for the use of codecs in the 'Advanced' properties. The choice of codec will affect the size of file but must be suitable for what the target video player will be.

Note: If footage is recorded in PAL on MiniDV and exported from the video editing software as HDV format, it will not have the same sharpness as genuine high-definition footage. If the detail was not recorded in the first place, you cannot put it back in later.

After you have exported the video, test the playback in a media player to make sure that the video is displayed correctly and that the sound volume is suitable for the intended use.

Using other software

The screen layout varies but the three basic sections in most software are:

1. Preview window
2. Tools or Task Panel
3. Timeline/Storyboard (usually at the bottom).

The basic processes and concepts of creating digital video are the same whatever software is being used. These are:

1. Capture the original footage (or import into a new project).
2. Save the video clips in a project file.
3. Arrange the clips on the Timeline.
4. Trim and cut clips as required.
5. Add transitions between clips.
6. Add title text.
7. Import a soundtrack or voiceover.
8. Export the final cut of the video in a suitable format.

When using different software for the first time, identify how to do the basics and then build your knowledge of the extra features as needed.

There are a number of other software options for video editing. A brief look at some of these is illustrated on the following pages.

Microsoft Movie Maker®

This is built into the Microsoft Windows® Operating System and provides the necessary features needed for video editing at this Level. The principles and approaches are the same as for Adobe Premiere Elements.

Video clips can be previewed in the window on the right-hand side. Imported media can be dragged and dropped onto the storyboard at the bottom of the screen. To add an audio track, select the Timeline from the View menu. Import your audio file and drag to the audio/music track.

Transitions between each video clip can be set using 'Edit' > 'Transitions' on the Task panel.

Titles and Effects can be added in a similar way, as shown below.

Publishing settings can also be set (shown for publishing to 'This Computer' as a target location).

Note that these settings give an option for the direct selection of what to compress the file size down to. Lower values for the bit rate and number of frames per second will reduce both the quality and file size. Test the playback of the exported file to make sure that the final video it is fit for purpose.

Adobe Premiere Pro CS3

Adobe Premiere Pro is a professional-level video editing software application. It includes a wide range of powerful editing tools.

The graphical user interface has a large number of panels to choose from for the type of video or audio editing required.

- The left-hand side includes panels for file/folder management.
- The workspace area displays a preview of the video, with playback controls and a timescale.
- The central area of the workspace is shown here with the audio editing controls.
- The main Timeline is shown at the bottom of the screen with multi-track video and audio.
- The bottom right-hand corner is shown with panels for editing tools and audio.

Pinnacle Studio 11

The workspace features an asset panel (top left), preview window (top right) and Timeline at the bottom of the screen.

- Three main tabs provide for capture, edit and export.
- There is a built-in music generator for audio soundtracks.
- The software supports a wide range of input formats including DivX® and AVCHD.
- Export formats include DivX, RealVideo® 8, Windows Media® 9 and MPEG-1, -2 and -4.

Apple iMovie

This video editing software application is part of the iLife suite.

The graphical user interface has the standard video preview window (left), media files panel (right) and a Timeline at the bottom.

- The software provides capture and editing modes.
- Panels are provided for clips, themes, media, editing and chapters.

- Timeline view has options for arranging video clips and adjusting the timing of the audio and video.

Other professional-level video editing applications for use on an Apple Mac computer are Final Cut Pro and Avid.

PART 4: REVIEWING DIGITAL VIDEO PROJECTS

1 Objective (4)

2 Objective (3d)

2 Objective (4a)

When reviewing your video project work, there will be a number of questions you need to ask:

1. Does the content of the final cut show what the client actually wanted?
2. Is the video file size suitable for the client and target audience?
3. Is the video file format suitable for the client and target audience?
4. Is the quality of the video footage suitable in terms of exposure, sharpness of focus, camera shake, colour, lighting and sound?
5. Is the video editing effective and pleasing to look at?
6. Are the transitions and audio mixing suitable?
7. Does the final work demonstrate a conventional or creative/innovative approach? There is no right or wrong here – just recognise what has been produced.
8. What improvements could be made – for example in equipment, video recording techniques and/or editing?

You may want to obtain some constructive comments from friends and the client in order to answer these questions. You could also refer to the general comments in the section on Planning and Review in the Introduction.

SUMMARY

In this unit we have covered video technology, use of a digital video camera and non-linear video editing. It is by developing skills with the use of a video camera and editing software that will enable you to create a wide range of video projects. Perhaps you will have experimented with camera movement and composition during the recording of your video footage. Remember that video editing techniques can be changed if something doesn't work but sometimes it can be difficult to go back and re-shoot a scene. Good-quality footage is the best foundation for producing high-quality video project work.

FINAL ASSIGNMENT

Once you have learned all the required parts of the unit, you will complete an assignment that will be used to assess your knowledge and skills of the subject. It will be set in a vocational context, which means that it will simulate what it would be like to be given a project by a client or employer in a work situation. To start you should read the brief or scenario carefully to identify what is needed. A typical assignment may be in the following format (although these should not be used as templates for designing your own assignments – refer to the guidance documents on the OCR website for this purpose):

> *Brief:*
> *You are a junior video technician for Tulipa Rossa sports goods and have been asked to produce a short video clip that can be used on their new website. For this you will need to record footage on a sporting theme, transfer it to a computer and edit it to create a 30-second video.*
> *Task 1: Here you may be asked to explore a range of appropriate video recording hardware, software and techniques along with the suitable file formats for the final work.*
> *Task 2: In this task you will be asked to plan the development of your work. Use one or more of the planning methods described in the Introduction, identifying what you will need*

and how long it is likely to take. A pre-production storyboard should be created before starting to record any footage.

Task 3: In this task you will be asked to actually produce or create your work. This should demonstrate a range of skills using the video camera and video editing software. You will also need to test the exported video file to make sure the file size/format is suitable for the client brief.

Task 4: In this task you should review your final work. This means thinking about things like overall quality, fitness for purpose and any areas for improvement. It is not just a summary of how you created the work – it should be a reflection by yourself (and others) on how suitable it is for use by the client described in the brief.

Note that essential parts of the assignment include the planning and reviewing of your work. It is important to be able to think about what you need to produce and what the final work should look like. Since the assignment is in a vocational context it will be important to check the suitability of what you have produced before submitting it to the client. The development of these skills will be a great benefit when you are asked to produce something in the real/commercial world of employment.

Computer Games

The aim of this unit is to learn how to use game engine software to create a playable computer game. It is assumed that the basic game concepts and structure have already been produced by a game designer and it is now necessary to develop those concepts into a playable game. This chapter covers both:

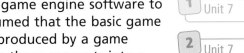

1 Unit 7

2 Unit 7

- Level 1 Unit 7 (Design and Test Games)
- Level 2 Unit 7 (2D Games Engines)

Types of games and gaming platforms are covered in more detail in the first part of the next chapter on game design. You will need to reference some of this information for your exploration of game types, components and platforms as part of the Level 1 unit.

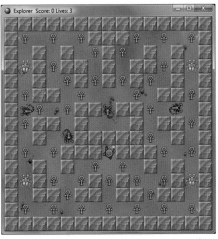

Gamemaker demo game

PART 1: EXPLORE AND REVIEW TYPES OF GAMES

1 Objective (1a)

2 Objective (1a)

For this objective you will review a number of games to identify their strengths and weaknesses. Before you start, you will need to list what you will be reviewing and decide on a rating system. Have a look through games magazines and at gaming websites to identify how they rate games and what they are looking for.

How to review a game

1 Objective (1b)

A review should recognise the type of game in addition to the player's experience of the game play. When reviewing games in this way, decide on a mark or score for each category, for example out of 5 stars or marks out of 10.

Name of Game	{insert name of the game being reviewed}
Platform	eg PC, Xbox, Wii, PlayStation etc
Description	First person role player adventure game. The player is a special agent and must find one of the entrances to the underground cavern where an alien race is building a machine to extract all of the oxygen from the planet.
Comments	Slow start to the game, where the player is roaming the city streets to find the entrance. More exciting once inside the cavern where the player must avoid being seen by the aliens until close enough to the oxygen extractor machine.
Gameplay (max 5 stars)	☆ ☆ ☆
Graphics	☆ ☆ ☆
Sounds	☆
Wow Factor	☆ ☆
Overall rating	☆ ☆ ☆

1. **Genre**
   1.1. What type of game is it? For example First Person Shooter (FPS), action, adventure, racing, puzzle, strategy.
2. **Game play**
   2.1. What does the player have to do?
   2.2. How difficult is the game to learn and play?
   2.3. What is the overall theme?
3. **Display graphics**
   3.1. Are the graphics detailed, high-resolution colour or very basic?
   3.2. Does the speed of the display 'feel' to be slow when changing views or moving?
4. **Sounds**
   4.1. What are the sound effects for? For example, background or actions/events.
   4.2. Are the sounds appropriate? For example, too long, too short, realistic or annoying.
5. **Interest**
   5.1. Is the game addictive – do you want to play a lot more?
   5.2. What levels of progression or upgrades exist to maintain interest?
6. **Accessibility**
   6.1. Is there any special hardware or interface devices required?
   6.2. Is the screen easy to read?
7. **Target audience**
   7.1. What is the age range and gender of people who are most likely to enjoy playing the game?

PART 2: PLANNING GAME DEVELOPMENT

1 Objective (3a)

2 Objective (2a)

The aim of the Level 2 unit (2D games engines) is to produce a playable computer game from a specification or client brief. This is one of the possible job roles in the game industry, where a game design has been created and now must be coded or created in the development software. Hence the visualization of the game will have already been produced by the games designer. This means there is not as much scope for creative ideas and planning of your own work here. For Level 2, it is important to recognise the client's requirements from a written brief/specification and/or discussion. At Level 1, you will develop the basic skills in creating a game using your game engine software.

For these units in particular, think about how long it will take to produce the game. You could break this down into timescales for:

- producing/obtaining assets
- creating the game world
- defining the game object properties and events
- game testing.

2 Objective (2b)

As one of the outcomes from testing at Level 2, you need to identify, plan and apply improvements to the game. This is one area where you can demonstrate planning methods and approaches, using the standard techniques explained in the section on Planning and Review in the Introduction. Areas for potential improvement could be:

Movement

Are the game controls suitable (e.g. use of keyboard/mouse or joystick)? Can movement be accurately controlled in both speed and direction? Could game play be improved by adding new movements such as jumping or running?

Scoring

Does the scoring system provide feedback to the player on how well they are doing? Could bonus points be obtained for extra achievement in the game? Is there a table of high scores to provide challenges between different players?

Interactions

These can be between the player and game objects or other game characters.

Obstacles

Consider the impact of increasing the number of obstacles so that the player has to develop more skills in moving around the game world. If a player has a sense of achievement by developing and using game skills, would the game be more interesting and/or successful?

Characters

Think about whether the game would benefit by adding more NPC (non-player characters)? These could be used to improve player interaction or increase the level of difficulty of the game.
Keep records of all sources and permissions obtained for any assets such as graphics or sounds used in the assessed game. The use of copyrighted, trademarked or intellectual property will need to be recorded in a standard format. An asset table is supplied on the CD for this.

PART 3: CREATING COMPUTER GAMES

Software options

Objective (2a)

Games can be coded using programming languages such as Visual Basic, C++ or Java. However, it is more likely that you will use a games editor or games engine to create a playable game. These provide a range of high-level functions that simplify the game creation process.

Games engine	Distributor	Description
Game Maker®	YoYo games	2D games engine with simple user interface
Mission Maker®	Immersive Education	3D games engine with drag-and-drop functionality. Can also be used for Level 1 and Level 2 when keeping to simple one- or two-room games
Games Factory®	Clickteam	Drag-and-drop games development functionality
Thinking Worlds	Caspian	3D games development engine that is free for non-commercial use

Many commercially available games are supplied with a 'level editor'. This enables you to create new levels and customise the game play. For the purposes of this unit though, you will most likely be creating a new game using a games engine rather than a customised level of a game using an editor. In general, a level editor will only allow you to modify or customise a game concept that already exists. A games engine will allow you to create a new game from scratch. Have a look at the games engine software that you have available. Find out information about the capabilities and features either from the manufacturers'/distributors' website or the built-in help.

Using Game Maker

Game Maker is a 2D games engine that is used to create a variety of computer games. Typical examples include racing, maze and strategy games.

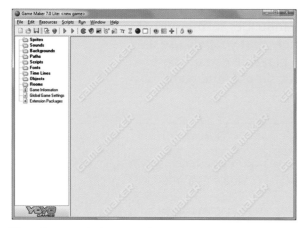

The Game Maker workspace

The Game Maker toolbar

A sprite is a small graphic or image that is used in the game. Within Game Maker, it is a graphic that represents the player or any other item in the game. These sprites are used to create game objects that can have events and actions associated with them.

Note: When using Game Maker to create games, do not use spaces in the names of sprites, objects and other game components. This is because of the way the programming code works and good practise is to use an underscore (_) instead of a space to make names more readable, for example 'player_object'.

Creating a new game

1 Objective (2b)

Creating the basics of a new game consists of six steps:

2 Objective (3a)

Step 1: Add sprites and set the properties

2 Objective (3b)

This is where you can import the graphics that will be used in the game. These graphics can be created using digital image editing applications such as those used in Chapter 2. In the OCR assignments and the example here, the graphics have already 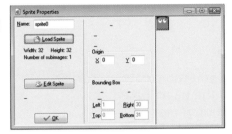 been created and saved at a size of 32 × 32 pixels. Click on the 'Add Sprite' button in the toolbar. The transparency check box determines whether the rectangular background of the sprite is a solid colour or transparent. Note that the colour of the pixel in the bottom left-hand corner is identified by Game Maker as the background colour, which is used to specify the colour that will be transparent.

Step 2: Add sounds

This is where you can import the sounds that will be used in the game. Click on the 'Add Sound' button in the toolbar. Click on the 'Load Sound' button to browse for the files stored on your computer. The recommended file format is .wav although .mp3 can be used as well. The potential issue with mp3 sounds is that they are in a compressed format and take more processing power to reproduce the sound playback (which could slow down the gameplay). When loading sounds, you can play the sound to check  that it is suitable. Type a descriptive name for the sound in the 'Name' field.

Step 3: Add a background

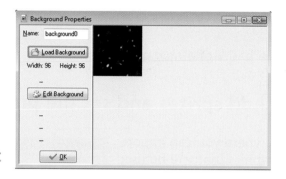

This is where you can load the background graphics or image for the game. Click on the 'Add Background' button in the toolbar.

Step 4: Add objects and set the properties/events

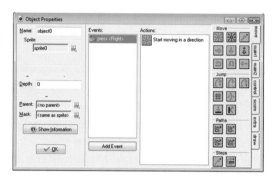

This is where you can create the events in the game based on the interaction of game objects. Click on the 'Add Object' button in the toolbar. Examples are movement, collisions, interactions, mouse/ keyboard control and scoring.

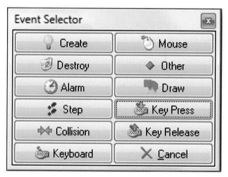

The name given to the object should describe what it is, so a suitable name here would be something like fish_obj. Most objects will be ticked to confirm that they are visible in the game although hidden objects, such as treasure, could be made invisible. Wall objects at the edge of the game room should be set to solid so that the player cannot move outside the room.

'Events' is where the game interactions are defined. To create movement, click on 'Add Event' and choose the type from the list.

- **Create** is used to start object movement or create other game events.
- **Keyboard, Key Press and Key Release** are used to control player movement based on the <left>, <right>, <up> and <down> keys in addition to other keys used for game control.
- **Collision** is used to control what happens when two objects collide e.g. for one of the objects to be destroyed.

The tabs along the right-hand side are: move, main1, main2, control, score and draw.

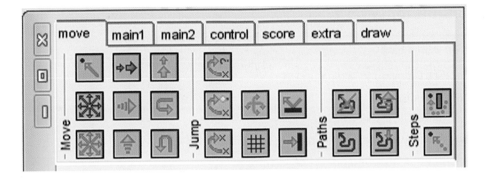

Note: This is rotated left for clarity.

Basic controls and actions

- **Movement:** Use the action to 'start moving in a direction' by dragging and dropping the icon from the right-hand side into the 'Actions' area. A window will be displayed for you to choose the direction of motion (select all eight arrows for a random direction). You can also change the speed from the default value of '8' if needed. To control the movement of the player object using the keyboard, you will need to define an action using 'Add Event' and 'Key Press'.
- **Collisions:** When an object such as the player sprite collides with another object, the result can be defined using an event, for example reversing the direction of movement and/or playing a sound.
- **Sounds:** From the 'main1' tab, drag the 'Play Sound' icon to the Actions window. You will be asked for a sound file name, otherwise the name will be left as <undefined>. A background sound, such as music, can be set to start with the game and loop continuously.
- **Scoring:** From the 'score' tab, drag 'set the score' to the Actions window. In the score properties, start with a value of '1' and 'relative'. This will add '1' to the current score whenever the previous action has completed.

Typical game controls for Level 1

1 Objective (2b)

Group tab	Action
Move	Move: Start moving in a direction
	Jump: Bounce against objects
Main2	Game: End the game (such as when the player object exits the level or dies)

Typical game controls for Level 2

Group tab	Action and category
Move	Move: Start moving in a direction
	Move: Set horizontal speed
	Move: Set vertical speed
	Move: Set the gravity (can be used in any direction)
	Move: Reverse horizontal direction
	Move: Reverse vertical direction
	Move: Set friction
	Jump: Jump to a position (given, random or start)
	Jump: Snap to grid
	Jump: Bounce against objects
Main1	Objects: Create an instance of an object
	Objects: Destroy the instance
	Sprite: Change the sprite
	Sounds: Play a sound
	Sounds: Stop a sound
	Rooms: Go to next room
	Rooms: Restart the current room
Main2	Timing: Sleep for a while (freezes the scene while information is displayed)
	Timing: Set an alarm clock (for timed events)
	Game: End the game (such as when the player object exits the level or dies)
Score	Score: Set the score

Step 5: Add a room

This is where you can define the size and shape of the game room. Although it is called a game room, it is really just a place where the game will be played and is not like a physical 3D room. Click on the 'Add room' button in the toolbar.

The main parameters for creating the room are found in the three tabs at the left-hand side of the room properties window:

- **Settings:** This sets the size (in pixels) of the room. This can be your display monitor pixel dimensions such as 640 × 480 or 800 × 600. The 'snap' settings define the spacing of the grid that is used to position objects in the room for the start of the game.

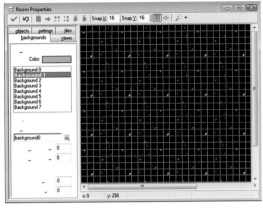

- **Backgrounds:** This allows you to choose a colour or image to be used for the game.
- **Objects:** This is where you can select which of the objects added to the game can be placed in the room. Select the object you want, such as a wall or rock object. Click around the edges of the room and any other locations to place the objects. The placing of the objects should be suitable for the properties and actions that were defined in Step 4.

1 Objective (2c)

2 Objective (3d)

Step 6: Play and test the game

You can test the game play using the 'Play game' button on the toolbar, which is the green 'play' arrow. Game Maker will build the game and display the game room ready to start play. If something does not work as planned, pressing the 'Escape' key will return you to the Game Maker development environment. Make any changes required and re-test the game.

Game testing

Apart from playing the game to get the best scores and fastest times, you need to thoroughly test all aspects of the game. For example, try colliding with a wall object to see if you disappear out of the room. You are not only testing and checking what should happen, but also what should *not* happen. A more detailed description of game testing is covered later in this chapter, after the introduction to Mission Maker below.

Two other considerations (before you save the final version of a game from Game Maker) are the game information and global game settings. You can find links to these on the toolbar or in the resource explorer at the left-hand side of the screen.

Game information

This tells the player how to play the game and will be displayed when they press the <F1> key. A basic set of instructions would include how to start and stop the game together with a short description of what they must do in the game world. Put your name at the bottom of the information window as the author of the game.

Global game settings

These enable you to change settings for graphics and display options, window shape, game control, error handling and version control.

Saving the game

The standard file format for Game Maker version 6.x has the file extension .gm6, but these files can only be opened and played in Game Maker. To distribute a game for others to play, select 'Create executable' from the 'File' menu. Choose a short name for the game that describes what it is. You may not be able to upload executable files to the e-Portfolio so always submit the original .gm6 or equivalent file with your work.

Using Mission Maker

Mission Maker is a high-level 3D 'drag and drop' games development environment developed by Immersive Education. Their website is at: http://www.immersiveeducation. co.uk.

Creating a new game in the editor

The process for creating a game in Mission Maker is very similar to Game Maker although the screen layout is very different. The sequence of steps in Mission Maker is:

1. Create the game world by adding locations and connecting them together with doors.
2. Add objects and props, set the properties and define actions.
3. Add or import sounds, set the properties.
4. Define all actions and triggers for events and interactions in the game.

5. Play, test and save the game.

Creating the game world

There are two drop-down menus for 'My Game' (top left) and 'New' (top right).

The first step in Mission Maker is to create a game environment or a location where the game will be set. Click on 'New' > 'Location'.

In the Game Editor, the rooms and passageways available can be seen along the top of the screen as tiles. These have already been created and stored in the Mission Maker library. They can be dragged into the game world, which is shown as a map. There are approximately ten different types of environment including science fiction, Western and Stone Age.

Each tile represents a 3D location that also has a number of doorways for connections to other locations. When you drag these onto the 2D grid (map view) they can be rotated by a single click until the doorways are in the positions that you want. Without these connected doors, you will not be able to move between two or more locations or rooms.

When all the locations are positioned as needed, you build your 3D world by clicking inside the pale blue box on the right-hand side of the screen. For creating games at Level 1 or Level 2, keep the game world quite

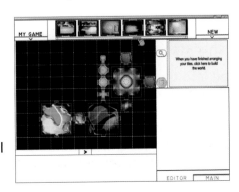

simple with just a few locations or rooms connected together. Even one room could be used if suitable game objects are also placed in it.

Set the properties of items and objects in the game

All items that have been added including the locations have properties that can be defined. In the lower right-hand corner, three tabs are provided:

- **Properties:** Used to set the lighting and sounds or acoustics in the location. If an object is 'Active', it will be displayed in the game world.
- **Actions:** Used to add audio effects, for example a door opening, or use triggers to change the lights.
- **Associations:** This provides a summary of how the location is linked to the rest of the game play.

Importing props and creating interaction

These add interest to the game world and help to define the visual style of the game. From the 'New' menu, click on 'Props' and select your objects from the top of the screen. As with the locations, Properties/Actions/Associations can be used to change the size, sounds and active status. On the 'Active' property, you will see a list of trigger types available. A trigger is an action that starts a new event or makes something happen. To keep things simple to start with, try the 'Object clicked' trigger. Using this action, a prop such as a box or door placed in the game world will be opened when the player 'clicks' on it with the mouse.

Creating game characters

These are imported into the game in the same way as other objects, using the 'New' menu and 'Character'. Drag and place the character in a chosen position in the game. The Properties, Actions and Associations are set for character objects in the same way as any other object. However, you have a wide range of options for editing the character in terms of walk style, head shape, torso (body) and legs. This allows you to mix and match the appearance of your game character(s).

Adding sounds

These are imported from the 'New' menu > 'Media' and then 'Audio'. A range of sound effects from the built-in library can be found at the top of the screen. You can also add your own mp3 sound files, sourced or created in other units. To use your own sound, click on the 'Filename' box in the Properties/Actions/ Associations panel and browse for the file on your computer. Set the properties to start/stop as needed or use a trigger from the 'Actions' tab.

Game and player attributes in Mission Maker

From the 'My Game' menu, these parameters set the objectives of the game and player.

For example, the timer countdown on the properties by default will countdown from 300 seconds. This can be used as a maximum time to complete the game level. The timer will run when the game is being played, but you must define an action to be triggered when the countdown reaches zero. Otherwise there is no time limit to the game.

The properties tab of the player attributes is used to set the player's initial health and how this changes as a result of game play.

Playing a game in Mission Maker

The game information is displayed at the bottom of the screen in four main sections:

- **Inventory:** Any item that is found and picked up in the game can be placed in the inventory. Just click on the item, and drag and drop it onto an empty inventory position.
- **Economies:** This includes a game timer, scores, health and nutrition.
- **Speech:** This displays speech text when characters talk in the game.
- **Camera/Player's log:** To record 'photographs' or images captured during game play.

Movement through the game world is controlled using the arrow keys and/or mouse. The arrow keys (or the letter keys WASD) can be used for forward, back, left and right. The right-click button on the mouse is used for up/down. Alternatively you can press and hold the scroll wheel of the mouse and move around the game world as needed.

Saving a game

At any time in the editor, you can select the 'Main' menu at the bottom of the Properties/Actions/Associations panel. Click on 'Save' and choose a name that describes the game you are creating. You can save a game as a .mission file or export the game as a .playmission file. It is suggested that your final game is exported because the e-Portfolio has a Mission Player built in.

The types of file are slightly different in that:

- To play a game using a '.mission' file, you need the full version of Mission Maker.
- To play a game using a '.playmission' file, you need Mission Maker Player, which is freely available.

Other software options

Games Factory 2

This is another type of games creation software provided by Clickteam. The processes involved in game creation are very similar to Game Maker and Mission Maker.

The screen layout is shown (right).

Games Factory 2 uses drag-and-drop editing techniques to create the game world. Game objects are placed in the game and actions created to define what happens. Graphics and sounds could be created as part of other units and imported into the game development software.

Testing of computer games

Whatever game engine software you are using, the aims and objectives of testing are the same. At this level testing is based on

playing the game to check the functionality of game play. There are two approaches to consider:

1. Functional testing to make sure that everything works correctly according to the original brief/specification.
2. General software testing to try and break or crash the game/computer.

The second approach is just as likely to find problems as the first, because the client brief/specification is not going to cover every possible situation. For example, have a few other software applications running in the background to see if the game or computer system becomes unstable. Try to get the player object out of the game world either by running or jumping at each room boundary. Using this approach, ignore the main objectives of the game play. Instead of shooting the monster, what happens if you try to blast your way through a fixed wall in the game room? This is one area where an imaginative and creative mindset can identify problems or unforeseen errors that would be missed by conventional approaches.

An example of a test plan is shown on the next page. It identifies what is being tested, the criteria used to decide on pass/fail and space to record the test result. When using a test plan and fixing the problems identified, always re-test the game in full to make sure that all aspects still work. With any software development, making one change to fix something can actually cause new problems somewhere else.

Test plan			
Test	Criteria for pass/fail	Pass/fail result	Errors/results
Player object shown in the game	Correct start position and viewpoint	✓	
Player object moves left	By pressing left arrow key on keyboard	✓	Quick response
Player object moves right	By pressing right arrow key on keyboard	✓	Quick response
Graphics are displayed and rendered correctly	Sprites transparent in the right places Lighting adequate to play the game	✓	Dark screen – difficult to see clearly
Game and computer system are stable	Did the computer or game crash during testing?	✓	
Speed of game play suitable	Any unreasonable delays, pauses or erratic movement. Is there a quick response to all key presses/game controls?	✓	
continued...			

Note: Comments may also be put into the pass/fail results column. The tests shown are general examples and you will need to define your own tests for the game created. This will also depend on what game engine software was used and also the rules/boundaries of the defined game.

Improvements to computer games

2 Objective (3e)

Having developed a functional game, the next objective for this unit is to identify areas for improvement. You may have found some of these at the game testing stage but consider what else could be improved. Some of the main areas were described in Part 2 of this chapter but you may have identified some additional opportunities to improve the game play as a result of testing. For the purposes of the assignment, you will need to plan and apply these game improvements.

PART 4: REVIEWING THE COMPUTER GAME

1 Objective (3b)

2 Objective (4a)

A review of a computer game must include detailed testing to make sure that the game works to specification. In addition to your own testing of the game, you may want to obtain some comments from friends and the target audience about the game play. This will help to recognise areas for further development, for example graphics quality, sounds and game objectives.

Identify any parameters and constraints that affected the creation of the game. These may include limitations of the game engine or the computer platform. If the game is slow, think about possible reasons such as large graphic or sound files. These can use up a large proportion of the computer system resources. Consider how these assets could be modified to keep the file size smaller, for example using different file formats or compression techniques. Instead of one long background sound, could a shorter section be used and looped so that it constantly replays?

SUMMARY

This chapter has introduced the techniques and processes of using game engine software to produce playable computer games. Starting from a detailed client specification, you will have imported graphics, objects and sounds into a games engine to create the game. You should have found that detailed testing of the game needs to be planned and completed thoroughly to make sure that everything works correctly. If a game player finds that a game doesn't work properly, they will often give up on it and find something else. Manufacturers have found this out to their own cost.

If you have also had some ideas for improving or developing a different game – have a read through the next chapter. Game design is the process of developing original ideas into innovative and creative new games. It is possible that the work completed for the games design unit could be used as the basis for creating the game in this computer game unit.

FINAL ASSIGNMENT

Once you have learned all the required parts of the unit, you will complete an assignment that will be used to assess your knowledge and skills of the subject. It will be set in a vocational context, which means that it will simulate what it would be like to be given a project by a client or employer in a work situation. To start you should read the brief or scenario carefully to identify what is needed. A typical assignment may be in the following format (although these should not be used as templates for designing your own assignments – refer to the guidance documents on the OCR website for this purpose):

> *Brief:*
> *You are a junior games developer for Tulipa Rossa games and have been asked to create a new game using the design document that has been supplied. This will be based on a player character that moves around a maze to collect five different items of sports equipment. When all the items have been found, the player will be able to exit the game room.*
> *Task 1: Here you may be asked to explore the features and capabilities of game engine software, identifying which will be most relevant for the client brief that has been supplied.*
> *Task 2: In this task you will be asked to plan the development of your work. Use one or more of the planning methods described in the Introduction, identifying what you will need and how long it is likely to take. Ideas for the creation of an improved game will also be needed here.*
> *Task 3: In this task you will be asked to actually produce or create the game. This will demonstrate your ability to use the game engine software to create a game from a clearly defined game specification. You will also need to test the finished game to make sure it works as described in the client brief.*
> *Task 4: In this task you should review your final work. This means thinking about things like overall quality, fitness for purpose and any areas for improvement. It is not just a summary of how you created the work – it should be a*

reflection by yourself (and others) on how suitable it is for use by the client described in the brief.

Note that essential parts of the assignment include the planning and reviewing of your work. It is important to be able to think about what you need to produce and what the final work should look like. Since the assignment is in a vocational context it will be important to check the suitability of what you have produced before submitting it to the client. The development of these skills will be a great benefit when you are asked to produce something in the real/commercial world of employment.

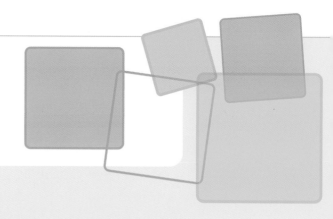

Game Design

This unit is about the process of designing a new game. You will learn about the core components of games and the capabilities of gaming platforms. Building on this knowledge, you will apply this to a game design brief in order to define the key concepts and components of a new game.

The games industry has a number of different roles:

- games designer
- games developer
- games tester
- software developer

Designers may have slightly different approaches to their work depending on who they actually work for. They may be:

1. designers of concept ideas for new games irrespective of platform
2. designers needed to develop new games for specific platforms.

If a games designer produces an idea for a new game, it could potentially be sold to a developer who has a specific platform in mind. This type of approach is independent of the hardware at the time the concept ideas are developed, although a general awareness of capabilities and specifications will be useful. This awareness may not restrict the ideas development but at least enable the designer to establish a realistic framework for the game play.

In the second example, games designers are more likely to be employed by a games platform manufacturer. Therefore, the games designer can develop ideas and concepts that can make the best use of the existing hardware capabilities.

The performance of any platform will be dependent on the electronic hardware. When developing a new game concept, it is no good attempting to render detailed and complex 3D scenes with small graphical displays and low-performance processors. If you do, the update speed of the display will be too slow and difficult to identify because the resolution will not be high enough. For the purposes of this unit you, as a games designer, will need to know the capabilities of the hardware on your chosen platform before deciding what the game will look like. So, in this first section we will look into the capabilities and features of gaming platforms.

The Nintendo Wii

PART 1: EXPLORING HARDWARE PLATFORMS AND GAME COMPONENTS

2 Objective (1a)

Choice of computer platforms

PC

A popular computer platform for both playing and developing digital games. Specifications vary considerably and the player's experience of the game could vary from one computer to another.

Apple Mac

Although a computer, this is rarely used for games. However, the use of Intel processors in Mac computers now means that they can run games that were originally designed for a PC.

Games console

This is a dedicated platform for playing digital games that connects to a television. The most popular consoles are the Sony PlayStation, Microsoft Xbox and Nintendo Wii. They connect to televisions for a large display of the game environment.

Microsoft Xbox

Portable devices

Portable devices include the Nintendo Game Boy, Nintendo DS and Sony PSP. These are smaller pocket-sized games consoles that can be easily carried around. The display size is more limited, although many still have a high-quality/resolution screen.

The Nintendo DS

Mobile phone/PDA

Increased graphics quality and processing power mean that mobile phones and PDAs can also now support games as a versatile all-in-one entertainment and communications device. Rather than a mobile phone with built-in games, some devices could even be considered as a gaming device with a built-in phone.

Hardware

Processor

Processing power will impact on the overall game performance and the player's experience of gameplay. Low-resolution 2D graphics will not need as much processing power as a real-time high-resolution 3D environment that is rendered for different lighting effects. The playback of background audio tracks and events sounds will also affect the work that the processor must do. For example, .mp3 files are relatively small file sizes but they are also in a compressed format that must be uncompressed in order to play back. This is another task for the processor to complete. Fast processors consume more power and may need cooling fans to keep them cool. This puts a significant load on portable battery-powered games platforms, so tends to be restricted to mains-powered computers and consoles linked to television screens.

Memory

Memory is the second most important component that will determine the player's experience of the gameplay in terms of performance. In a computer system memory is used as a temporary storage area and has fast access when compared to a hard disk. If the computer system does not have enough memory installed it can use the hard disk for temporary storage instead, but the speed of access can slow down the overall gameplay.

Sound cards

Standard sound cards only drive two speakers, which would normally be placed in front of the player. For improved audio effects during gameplay, a sound card that supports 3D surround sound produces a more realistic experience for the player to feel that he/she is actually inside the game.

Graphics controllers

Real-time 3D graphics can use display technologies that are built into graphics controller cards. Using Microsoft Shader® technologies, the rendering of textures and lighting in a 3D scene is performed by the graphics card instead of the main computer CPU. This enables movie-quality visual effects in computer game environments. Advanced graphics cards and controllers have larger video memory and support DirectX 9.0 Shader Model 3.0 and NVIDIA® CineFX™ for example.

Display devices – types and specifications

CRT

This is a cathode ray tube and a typical display used on desktop computers. Standard sizes range from 15 to 21 inches.

LCD and plasma screens

Liquid crystal displays are used on laptop computers and can be supplied as flat panel monitors for use with desktop computers. Portable games consoles always use this type of display because it is very thin (unlike CRT displays). Plasma screens are typically 42 inches or larger and some have a high-definition television built in. This type of display can be used with games consoles such as Microsoft Xbox, Sony PlayStation and Nintendo Wii.

Resolution

The sharpness and perceived image quality of a display depends on the resolution, dot pitch and physical size of the screen. The resolution is determined by the number of pixels or dots that make up the display. This is quoted as width times height, for example 1024 × 768, which is also referred to as XGA. Other standard resolutions used on computer displays are:

Standard	Resolution	Aspect ratio
VGA	640 × 480	4:3
SVGA	800 × 600	4:3
XGA	1024 × 768	4:3
SXGA	1280 × 1024	4:3
SXGA+	1400 × 1050	4:3
WVGA	852 × 480	16:9
WXGA	1366 × 768	16:9
WXGA	1280 × 800	16:10*
WXGA+	1440 × 900	16:9

Note: Some newer laptops have aspect ratios of 16:10

Dot pitch

This is the spacing between the dots on the display screen. A closer spacing will enable a sharper image with typical values between 0.2mm and 0.3mm. This value is related to the resolution of the display and the physical size, that is, a high resolution on a smaller screen will have a lower value for the dot pitch (so that the dots are closer together).

RGB colour

A display screen is made up from three colour components – red, green and blue. Each colour has a number of bits that effectively define what shade of red it will be (or green or blue). So 8-bit colour will give 256 different shades of each, which equates to 24-bit colour display (using binary 2^8, which equals $2 \times 2 \times 2 \times 2 \times 2 \times 2 \times 2 \times 2$). This 24-bit depth produces a lifelike colour display of 16.7 million colours. Simple older types of games may use less than this in order to keep the display speed realistic for the game play.

Refresh rate

This refers to how quickly a CRT screen is updated. If the screen appears to flicker, the refresh rate may be too slow. LCD displays have a response time, which is the time taken to change a pixel from black to white and back to black again. Typical values are between 2 and 10 milliseconds (ms); faster response times give a smoother transition of graphics.

Storage media

Hard disk

The hard disk is the part of a computer system that stores the operating system and application software. If a computer game is installed from CD/DVD, the installation files and playable game will be saved onto the hard disk.

Games cartridges

The popularity and use of games cartridges has declined in recent years in favour of other formats. Some games consoles used this type of device, which was pre-loaded with a playable game. Every time the game was to be played, the cartridge was inserted into the console.

CD/DVD ROM

New computer games are often supplied on CD or DVD for installation to the hard disk. Where games have extended graphics, video or sounds, they are more likely to be supplied on DVD due to the higher storage capacity.

Blu-Ray

The Blu-Ray disc format is used by Sony on the PlayStation console and is the competitor for HD-DVD format. The Blu-Ray disc format can store 25GB of information, enabling high-quality graphics, video, sounds and extensive game play.

HD-DVD

HD-DVD is used by Microsoft on the Xbox 360 and is the competitor to the Blu-Ray format. It can store up to 15GB of information.

Flash memory

This is an electronic memory storage system that 'remembers' information after the power has been removed. It can be used to store games on portable devices and mobile phones.

Interface devices

Keyboard

Computer keyboard arrow keys are typically used to control movement but other keys are also used, such as W-A-S-D for left-handed people. Portable devices and mobile phones may have programmable function keys in addition to multi-rockers or jog dials.

Mouse

The mouse is a standard interface device for use with a computer system. Movement can be controlled by pushing the mouse forward or backward. Doors and other objects can be opened or used by clicking on them with the mouse pointer.

Paddle

A paddle is a controller used on early games platforms with a small wheel or paddle that is manipulated to control the player movement. Buttons are also included for actions in the game such as 'Shoot'.

Keypad/gamepad controller

This is a hand-held game controller used with games consoles. It provides more functions than a simple paddle with movement typically being controlled using the thumbs.

Joystick

A joystick is a popular game controller for use with flying, whether flight simulation or air-to-air combat. Buttons to fire

missiles and guns are found using the thumb and fore finger respectively.

Wheels

Wheels are used in driving or racing games to navigate a vehicle around a track. This simulates the normal method of vehicle control.

Pedals

Pedals are used in racing games to control speed or acceleration in the same way as in a car. They are used in conjunction with a wheel for directional control.

Motion detector

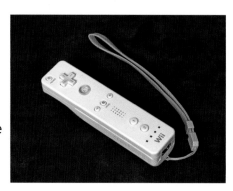

This is a hand-held controller that detects acceleration or movement in several directions. This is a relatively new type of game controller that enables a new type of gameplay as found on the Nintendo Wii.

Force feedback

This is a technology developed to simulate the response on the joystick or wheel that a player should experience in real life. Small motors are used in the game controller to respond to what is happening in the game and provide appropriate feedback to the player. It is typically used with wheels and joysticks.

PRACTICE EXERCISE

Research and review games platforms

1. Collect some information on games platforms, for example PC, Microsoft Xbox, PlayStation, Nintendo Wii Game Boy.
2. Compare the hardware features of each platform.
3. List what games are available for the platforms and whether any are multi-platform.
4. Compare the minimum system requirements for a range of computer games, such as processor speed, memory, sound and graphics.

Exploring Games

2 Objective (1b)

Many games will use a basic three-act structure in a very similar way to films and movies.

	Act 1	Act 2	Act 3
Movie	Story introduction	Main action	Story concludes
Game	Game introduction	Main game play	Final challenge

By combining a series of levels with increasing difficulty, a larger game can be produced. Each level may still follow the three-act structure but the increasing difficulty will satisfy the need for achievement and success in the game.

Components of a game

Objectives

These are what the player needs to achieve or complete as part of the game play. They can be mini-objectives as part of a level or the overall main objective for the whole game. The achievement of mini-objectives helps to engage the player and maintain interest throughout the game. It can form an important part of progression to the next level.

Act 1: Scene Introduction

Act 2: Gameplay
- find treasure
- renew health
- solve challenges

Act 3: Defeat monster

Environment/terrain

This means the visual style:

- look and feel of the environment
- challenge of the playing space
- atmospheric effects, for example mist and rain
- lighting – darkness
- form and scale – enclosed, claustrophobic, open.

Game play

Genre

The use of the term 'genre' in game terminology is sometimes slightly different to the traditional movie genre. For example, a first-person shooter (FPS) game could be created as a movie genre of the 'wild west' or 'science fiction'.

Genre	Examples (some of which fall into more than one category)
Action/Adventure	Half Life 2 Tomb Raider
Arcade	Space Invaders Asteroids
Card and board games	Solitaire Monopoly
Educational	Big Brain Academy
First-person shooter (FPS)	Doom Halo Star Wars – Jedi Knight
Historical	Age of Empires
Massively multiplayer online (MMO)	World of Warcraft
Puzzle	Maze games Solitaire
Racing	Grand Theft Auto
Role Playing (RPG)	Dungeons and Dragons Tomb Raider
Shoot 'em up	Space Invaders
Simulator	Flight Simulator
Sport	Tennis games Football games
Strategy	Sim City Age of Empires

Emotional themes

This relates to what the motivation is for the player in the game. It could be based on fear, revenge or valour. Is the main character trying to escape from something in order to survive or searching for something to save the world? These two approaches are likely to motivate different types of people, which may affect who the target audience is.

Narrative (storyline)

A game that has a strong narrative is said to have a very definite storyline. There is a clear purpose and reason for the character play. Games with a strong narrative include many role player (RPG), first-person shooter (FPS) and action/adventure. Genres such as racing or puzzle generally do not have a strong narrative. As a designer you will need to consider whether your target audience will like games with a strong narrative. Alternatively, the immediate satisfaction of winning a racing game or solving a puzzle could be more appealing.

Characters

These can be player characters (PC) or non-player characters (NPC). Examples of character types for the player include hero/heroine, villain, super-hero or god. Sim City and Sim Earth are examples of games where the player takes on a god-like role in the development of the city or planet. When you develop your sketches and drawings for characters, remember that a player will want to protect their own characters.

> **Game Characters**
> - Human/animal/monster
> - Size/shape
> - Clothing
> - Strength/ability
> - Protection/health
>
> Use concept art and sketches to show what they look like

A non-player character is any character in the game that is not controlled by a player. These characters' actions are determined by the game programmer when creating the game. Multi-player games allow more than one player and characters may take on different roles or even different sides. Players can often choose between being a hero or villain on opposite sides to each other. Alternatively, they may compete side by side in order to reach a certain goal. Racing would be a good example of this. Multiple players may share the same computer or play over a local area network. In MMO (massively multiplayer online) games, each player connects to the game using the Internet. In many of these games the players compete against each other using their own gaming skills. The desire to win against a 'real' opponent makes the games more addictive.

Interactions

The game play will involve a series of interactions with other characters and items in the game world. This could relate to a discussion or confrontation with another character. Alternatively, the narrative (storyline) may list a series of actions and events that the player must complete in order to finish the level. A simple example would be the opening of a door with a key – but where does the key come from? If the key is originally protected by another character and must be found, then a series of interactions are created that begin to define the game play.

Rules

Although referred to as the rules this is more the mechanics of the game, such as whether achievement is based on luck, tactics or skill. The outcome of a certain action can be decided by the roll of a dice or otherwise it can be a randomly generated result. The term 'rules' can also be used to describe whether the game meets 'real world' or 'fantasy world' rules. For instance, this could refer to the effect of gravity or the use of magical powers.

Scoring systems

These are a way to measure the player's progress through the game. Points can be obtained by achieving the game objectives in addition to bonus points for extra ability or achievements. In some games the achievement of high-value points can be used to gain extra lives or upgrades.

Sounds and audio

These enhance the gaming experience for the player. Background sounds help to create a realistic environment and create an atmosphere and overall 'feel' for the game. Other sounds can be used for events, actions and characters, for example using a laser blaster, opening a door and characters talking.

Target audience

Simple language, softer characters and/or cartoons are found in fun games designed for young (and old) people. Violence and bad language are often found in games played by teenage audiences although these would normally be considered as adult-themed games.

Accessibility

This refers to how people with disabilities could interact with the game. There are several areas to consider, such as interaction control (keyboard, joystick, and so on), visual and audible feedback to the player. Think about players who may have a visual impairment. Would they be able to identify and recognise crucial visual elements in the game, or would it be much harder for them to achieve the same scores as those with normal vision. Similar consideration of the audio part of a game can identify whether a hearing-impaired person would be disadvantaged by not being able to hear certain sounds.

Addiction

A game may be good to play once but this component of game design considers whether the player will want to come back and play again and again. Think about what key elements will ensure that players are motivated and keen to get back to the game world. The prospect of a challenge, achievement and upgrades in the game will help to increase the level of addiction. However, you will still need to know your target audience in order to know what will appeal to them.

PART 2: PLANNING THE DESIGN PROCESS FOR A DIGITAL GAME

Planning a game design for a client brief

2 Objective (2a)

For this game design unit the client brief will only set some broad context or reasons for wanting you to design a new game. Think about what options exist for satisfying the needs of the client and designing an interesting and creative new game at the same time. In this unit you will need to develop and use your own personal creative talents. In some ways the planning for this unit will be the whole design process because you will be planning the design of a new game without actually creating it.

Your general planning techniques will need to include a range of concepts and visualization sketches. You may also need to storyboard the narrative or game play to illustrate what happens as the player progresses through the level. Refer to the section on

Planning and Review in the Introduction for more general information on these techniques, which includes references on how to conceptualize, visualize and storyboard your work.

You will need to document any use of copyrighted, trademarked or intellectual property, whether this belongs to the client or somebody else. Keep records of all sources and permissions obtained for any material that is not your own. You may also need model and/or property releases from people and property that may be identified in your work.

Finally, think about how long the whole project will take. After your initial discussions with the client, they will want to know how long it will take to produce the work. Break this down into timescales for designing the game play, characters and narrative.

Game Design Plan	Mon	Tue	Wed	Thu	Fri
Identify suitable games platform	▬				
Develop/describe game objectives		▬			
Develop concepts of gameplay			▬		
Character design including non player characters			▬▬		
Develop narrative/storyline				▬	
Identify sounds used in the game				▪	
Produce portfolio for the new game design		▬▬▬▬			
Obtain client feedback				▪	
Review final work and list improvements					▪

Using game engines and editors

These can be used to test ideas and environments of game play to simulate what the game might look like. Depending on whether your game will be in 2D or 3D, a suitable game engine or editor must be chosen that can illustrate the basic ideas. Some examples of these are shown below, further details of which can be found in the previous chapter on computer games.

- Mission Maker
- Game Factory 2
- Game Maker
- Scratch
- Flash

Other software applications that could be used to support the development process include digital graphics editors. These can be used to draft the game backgrounds, scenes, environment and characters. If graphics for objects and characters are saved in a suitable size, resolution and format, they can also be assets that could be supplied to a games programmer. These can then be used in the games engine development application to create the game.

PART 3: DESIGNING A DIGITAL GAME

2 Objective (3a)

2 Objective (3b)

When designing a digital game your main steps are:

1. Describe the game concept.
2. Identify the target platform.
3. Identify the target audience.
4. Specify the genre.
5. Develop the game environment and narrative.
6. Develop the game characters.
7. Identify the sounds needed.

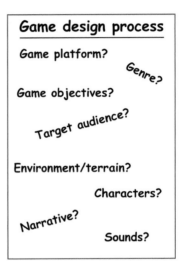

Developing a game concept

This diagram shows the initial concept at the centre and how the main components are linked around it. Spider diagrams or mind maps together with concept sketches are a good way to start the design process for a new game. These sketches may be of the game characters or what the terrain will look like. You can put a series of these together as a storyboard to illustrate the game play, as mentioned in the previous section.

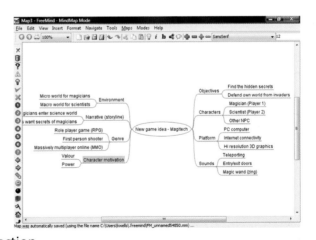

As a game designer you will also need to keep notes of all your ideas. Carry this around all the time to keep records of research, thoughts and experiences. Anything and everything can be noted down – it doesn't matter how wild and wacky the ideas are. In fact, the best designer notebooks will contain the best and worst of everything, but this can be organised later when going through the actual game design process.

The following is an extract from a game designer's notebook. . .

Thought about borrowing some ideas from another game so will have bigger guns, not one barrel but at least six. Maybe 32 barrels and the gun is eight feet high. Enjoyed playing Worms – so rather than bullets or shells maybe it fires heat seeking ducks with subspace plasma warheads (dunno what a plasma warhead is yet but will think of something). Nanotechnology is all in the news so probably need to make available a nanobot (nanotechnology robot). A new weapon – genetically modified cream cakes that dissolve anything on contact (fab idea developed after watching Alien and fresh food advert in between). Most games seem to work on a similar scale – so will do something different. In my new game, one race of people will be on a completely different scale to the other so that they cannot even see them. Macro and micro worlds – but how to interact between them? Maybe that's where the nanobot comes in. Superman was on TV earlier – the kryptonite rock that took away all his strength is an interesting idea. In my micro world, maybe there should be a super secret all-powerful crystal, rock or pebble that holds the secret to the subspace universe. It could have a core of dark matter – the blackest of all substances. Hmmm – if the most powerful device in the whole universe was spinning at the speed of light it could be invisibly small, have infinite mass and time would stand still. Perhaps a quest to find the 'pebble of darklight' is key to the survival of one species – the smallest ones at that. The greatest power comes from the smallest of things and the hurricane was borne from the flap of a butterfly's wings (chaos theory).

Need a graviton accelerometer and sub-atomic particle pulveriser. Could develop a solar energy body suit that is recharged in 2 hours of bright sunlight. Mission duration of 12 hours darktime at full power, which allows levitation and narrow band directional electromagnetic pulses (EMP).

How about another esoteric device that opens up the power of the human mind? If we only use around 10% of brain power, something in the game could be used to tap into the other 90% – but what does it do (or is that the aim of the game to find out?) Probably some sort of first-person, role-player game would be good to search for something like this. Finding the device would be the gateway to the next level – where the game rules change completely in terms of what is possible.

Science versus the magicians – 'Science built the Titanic but faith built the Arc'. Who would win such an epic duel?

Creativity in game design

Another extract from a game designer's notebook. . .

Somebody asked me where I get my ideas from and whether I could go through the ideas development process. Okay – so I look around my desk – I have a pen, paper clips, old battery and some music CDs. What can be made of them? First thought is that they are not ordinary items – by sheer fluke the steel that went into my pen came from a very special rock that had been squashed by a particular meteor that hit the earth 60 million years ago. During the impact it was heated to over 10,000°C but the live organisms were protected for a crucial few microseconds by the cosmic energy from the meteor that had passed through the alpha-omega nebulae over 3,000 light years away. Aha – now we have some potential. Unfortunately the paper clip is just a paper clip, but should the bacteria on it ever come into contact with the extra terrestrial life energy embedded in the pen within 10cm of the vapour given off by a dud battery. . . then we have three magic ingredients: bacteria, chemicals and energy! Marvel comics often used a similar process for the transformation of humans to have special powers. So ideas development is all about moving your thoughts from the ordinary to the extraordinary.

Creativity in any field – especially games design – comes down to going through life with a new set of eyes. Those eyes are the ones that you already have, but just see things differently. Anything that you see or do in real life can be combined to create something new. Maybe somebody else has already thought of it – but it is not possible that somebody somewhere has thought of everything, anywhere through the eternity of time. The stimulus for a new idea can be anything – if you want to try something new, go onto the Wikipedia website and do a search on a random article – then think something up for it.

Example of a new game design

2 Objective (3c)

This is not a detailed example of a game design but illustrates some of the steps and processes involved. Depending on the role and position of the game designer, the sequence of steps may differ in the real world, but the concepts can be easily adapted. Using the ideas from the designer's notebook earlier in this chapter, let's put these into a framework that includes the essential game components.

Step 1: Describe the game concept

- **Game description:** Magic versus technology – the ultimate confrontation? Game title will be Magicology or Magitech. Game concept will be 'Spells versus science'
- **Game objectives:** Obtain each other's secrets, protect own world. . .

Step 2: Identify the target platform

The concept of the game will need to be played online, with players taking each side and competing against each other. So, either a PC or Mac-based computer with an Internet connection will be required. It will need the capability to use portable wireless games platforms to connect with Wi-Fi using wireless hot spots. Many trains, pubs and hotels have hotspot connections so players could possibly connect and identify other players who are nearby. This would automatically allow these players to meet in the game environment, whether on the same side or opposite. This adds a sense of realism to the game play – to know that your opponent could be only a few metres away!

Step 3: Identify the target audience

The target audience will be broad, from early teens through to adults of both sexes. Different personalities and types of people could be motivated to choose one side or the other, for example scientists or magicians. They could be inspired by the challenge of competition as well as the achievement of success.

Step 4: Specify the game genre

The genre is first-person role-player game (FPRPG) as well as being MMO (massively multiplayer online).

Step 5: Develop the game environment and narrative

Magicians could be in a micro (tiny) world – and there could also be technology in a macro (normal size) world, creating nanodroids and nanobots to enter the lair of the sorcerer and his (or her) apprentice. The access points to the alternate worlds would need to be clearly identified and different in each case. The technology world would have scanning devices to search for entry points. These could even scan inside the micro-world to identify what sort of opponent or challenges they are likely to face. In this way, the player can choose their own missions to some extent.

Step 6: Develop the game characters

Develop some names for key characters in the game. Consider using anagrams of key words, where the same letters are used but in a different order, for example using the word 'magic' and moving the letters around we could have character names such as 'Cagim' or 'Gamic'.

- Anagram of 'magician' – Ganicaim
- Anagrams of 'technology' – Gotychonel, Logonetchy, Chetolygon (or split this into Cheto and Lygon)
- Anagram of 'science' – Sicecen
- Anagram of 'logic' – Golic

So the leader of the magicians will be Gamic and the players will be Ganicaims. The leader of the technology people will be Cheto and the players will be Lygons. Sicecen, Golic and Cagim will be non-player characters that the players interact with.

Of course in a real game design, character names could be made up from anything but rather than start with a blank sheet of paper, pick a word at random from the dictionary and see what you can come up with.

Character design is another important aspect. In the diagram (above) a concept character has been developed using Mission Maker.

Step 7: Identify the sounds needed

Sounds are needed for the drone of the nanodroid, and searching and scanning the micro-world. Sounds are also needed for the casting of a magic spell 'Zeeeiing' and the use of technology weapons 'Kerrboom'.

Step 8: Consider testing needs and appeal to the target audience

2 Objective (3d)

Testing needs

This will need to cover basic game play on a stand-alone computer from both sides, such as:

- preparation and launch of a nanodroid
- searching for a micro-world entry point
- transit into the micro-world
- search, seek and obtain secrets, eliminating opponents
- magician's world – use of magic wand to open portholes into the macro-world
- conjure up monsters and beings with special powers, sizes and shapes
- fly through a porthole into the macro-world to sabotage the launch of nanodroids (small size should make them invisible unless. . .)

Appeal

The two sides aspect of the game opens the appeal up to a much broader market sector, both male and female. The competitive nature of opponents who may be nearby will add an extra excitement factor.

PART 4: REVIEWING YOUR DIGITAL GAME

2 Objective (4a)

One of the most significant factors is whether your game design could be a commercial success. This means considering whether the needs of the client have been met and whether the game concept will appeal to a large number of people. Feedback from friends and needs of the client have been met and whether the game concept will appeal to a large number of people. Feedback from friends and the client will be an essential step in reviewing the game concept that has been designed.

Consider the following questions when reviewing your work:

1. Does the concept of the game design meet what the client actually wanted?
2. Is the game design suitable for the client's purposes and the target audience?
3. Is the narrative and genre suitable for the client's purposes?
4. Does the game design differ from existing games on the market? Are there any unique or innovative ideas? At this level the main aim is to recognise what has been produced and whether the work represents new and creative thinking.
5. What improvements could be made, for example game platform, game narrative, environment and terrain, character types/appearance and sounds?

SUMMARY

In this unit you will have learned what game components are essential to create a new game. This includes how to plan and use a structured design process with ideas and inspiration that is developed over a period of time. You will need to consider the client and a target audience for the game throughout the design to ensure that their expectations will be met. A review of the games platforms and their capabilities should ensure that realistic game concepts are designed for the hardware that will be available. The work you produce for this unit may be used as the basis for a game that is created for 'Game Engines' – subject to the approval of your teacher.

FINAL ASSIGNMENT

Once you have learned all the required parts of the unit, you will complete an assignment that will be used to assess your knowledge and skills of the subject. It will be set in a vocational context, which means that it will simulate what it would be like to be given a project by a client or employer in a work situation. To start you should read the brief or scenario carefully to identify what is needed. A typical assignment may be in the following format (although these should not be used as templates for designing your own assignments – refer to the guidance documents on the OCR website for this purpose):

> Brief:
> You are a junior games designer for Tulipa Games and have been asked to develop some ideas for a new game based on sporting equipment. The style and type of game is open to interpretation and the target platform must be identified in your work.
> Task 1: Here you may be asked to explore a range of target platforms. The capabilities of the display graphics and player interface controls must be reviewed to make sure they are suitable for the game proposal.
> Task 2: In this task you will be asked to plan the development of your work. Use one or more of the planning methods described in the Introduction, identifying what you will need and how long it is likely to take.
> Task 3: In this task you will be asked to produce your game design (but not create a playable game). The game design will describe a range of game components such as main objectives, characters, environment and genre.
> Task 4: In this task you should review your final work. This means thinking about things like overall quality, fitness for purpose and any areas for improvement. It is not just a summary of how you created the work – it should be a reflection by yourself (and others) on how suitable it is for use by the client described in the brief.

Note that essential parts of the assignment include the planning and reviewing of your work. It is important to be able to think about what you need to produce and what the final work should look like. Since the assignment is in a vocational context it will be important to check the suitability of what you have produced before submitting it to the client. The development of these skills will be a great benefit when you are asked to produce something in the real/commercial world of employment.

Index

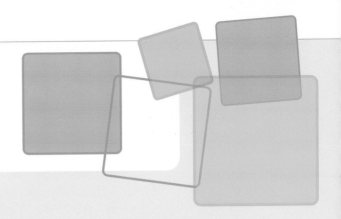